W9-CEK-487

3 1257 01854 7017

MODERN WORLD NATIONS

AFGHANISTAN	ISRAEL
ARGENTINA	ITALY
AUSTRALIA	JAMAICA
AUSTRIA	JAPAN
BAHRAIN	KAZAKHSTAN
BANGLADESH	KENYA
BERMUDA	KUWAIT
BOLIVIA	MEXICO
BOSNIA AND HERZEGOVINA	THE NETHERLANDS
BRAZIL	NEW ZEALAND
CANADA	NIGERIA
CHILE	NORTH KOREA
CHINA	NORWAY
COLOMBIA	PAKISTAN
COSTA RICA	PERU
CROATIA	THE PHILIPPINES
CUBA	PORTUGAL
DEMOCRATIC REPUBLIC OF THE CONGO	PUERTO RICO
EGYPT	RUSSIA
ENGLAND	SAUDI ARABIA
ETHIOPIA	SCOTLAND
FRANCE	SENEGAL
REPUBLIC OF GEORGIA	SOUTH AFRICA
GERMANY	SOUTH KOREA
GHANA	SPAIN
GREECE	SWEDEN
GUATEMALA	TAIWAN
HONDURAS	THAILAND
ICELAND	TURKEY
INDIA	UKRAINE
INDONESIA	THE UNITED STATES OF AMERICA
IRAN	UZBEKISTAN
IRAQ	VENEZUELA
IRELAND	VIETNAM

Saudi Arabia

Second Edition

Robert A. Harper
University of Maryland
with additional text by Aswin Subanthore

Series Editor
Charles F. Gritzner
South Dakota State University

CHELSEA HOUSE
PUBLISHERS
An imprint of Infobase Publishing

Frontispiece: Flag of Saudi Arabia

Cover: Muslim pilgrims pray inside Masjid al-Haran, the sacred mosque, in Mecca.

Saudi Arabia, Second Edition

Copyright © 2007 by Infobase Publishing

Chelsea House
An imprint of Infobase Publishing
132 West 31st Street
New York NY 10001

Library of Congress Cataloging-in-Publication Data
Harper, Robert Alexander.
 Saudi Arabia / Robert A. Harper with additional text by Aswin Subanthore. — 2nd ed.
 p. centimeters — (Modern world nations)
 Includes bibliographical references and index.
 ISBN-13: 978-0-7910-9516-4 (hardcover : alk. paper)
 ISBN-10: 0-7910-9516-9 (hardcover : alk. paper) 1. Saudi Arabia—Juvenile
literature. I. Subanthore, Aswin. II. Title. III. Series.

 DS204.25.H37 2007
 953.8—dc22   2007014922

Series design by Takeshi Takahashi
Cover design by Joo Young An

Printed in the United States of America

Bang NMSG 10 9 8 7 6 5 4 3 2 1

This book is printed on acid-free paper.

All links and Web addresses were checked and verified to be correct at the time of publication. Because of the dynamic nature of the Web, some addresses and links may have changed since publication and may no longer be valid.

Table of Contents

1   Introducing Saudi Arabia   8

2   Physical Landscapes   20

3   Life in the Desert   35

4   People and Culture   46

5   Government and Politics   59

6   Saudi Arabia's Economy   68

7   Regions of Saudi Arabia   89

8   Saudi Arabia Looks Ahead   99

    Facts at a Glance   105
    History at a Glance   108
    Glossary   110
    Bibliography   112
    Further Reading   113
    Index   115

Saudi Arabia

Second Edition

Introducing
Saudi Arabia

Suppose you are a camel herder in the desert. You and your relatives live in a tent camp. You have no electricity, no plumbing, and you cook over an open fire. You have never seen a train or an automobile. You live mostly on camel's milk and dates. You cannot read or write. Because you are deeply religious, your children are taught how to live strictly according to God's law—a law that does not accept change easily.

Your life centers on finding water and food for your camels. In your search you move camp every few weeks. You have no radio, no television, and no telephone. Your only contact with the outside world comes when you visit town to sell your camels and buy some supplies, or when you meet other tribes at a well.

WHAT TO DO WHEN YOUR TRIBE STRIKES IT RICH
Suddenly, outsiders who have different customs and clothes and speak a different language arrive at your camp. They offer you more

money than you have ever seen to let them drill for oil in your part of the desert. The deal includes a payment for every barrel of oil they produce.

You agree. The strangers arrive with machines you have never heard of: trucks and drilling equipment, even an airplane. They do not want to live in your tent communities, and you do not want them to, either. They build their own communities with their own types of houses and buildings, streets and cars, and their own food and lifestyle.

Not only do the outsiders find oil, but they discover that the largest supply of oil in the world lies under your land. At the same time, the demand for oil in the world explodes. Oil powers planes, ships, and cars; it helps pave roads; it is made into chemicals, plastics, and fertilizers; and it powers electric plants. More people throughout the world begin to use oil products. Oil production from your land increases each year. More foreign workers, with their different ways, arrive. Some of their ways you like, but some you do not.

Huge amounts of money roll in, not just to your country, but to you and your tribe. What are you, who never even had a bank account, going to do with this fortune?

You have money to buy anything your family wants; your nation can build cities, electric plants, water and sewage systems, roads, and airports. You can send all the children of your country to school for free; you can provide health care to everyone. What is not clear is how it should be done. How can it be done if you still wish to keep the religious, tribal, and family values you treasure?

OIL MONEY: THE DILEMMA OF THE HOUSE OF SAUD

This story is not the plot of a Hollywood movie. It is a problem that has faced the family that rules the country of Saudi Arabia since World War II (1939–1945). The money has brought not only great benefits, but also terrible problems and responsibilities. Massive changes have been made. There have been mistakes and there has been waste. The family was totally

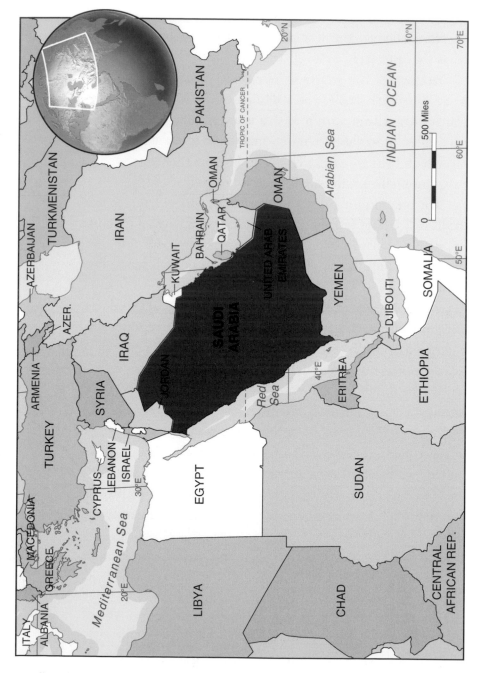

Saudi Arabia is located in the Middle East, between the Red Sea and the Persian Gulf. It shares borders with eight countries—Jordan, Iraq, and Kuwait, to the north; Yemen and Oman, to the south; and the United Arab Emirates, Qatar, and Bahrain, to the east—and is approximately one-fifth the size of the United States.

unprepared for the windfall of riches. Yet, it has made decisions that have changed the country. Today there are few wandering nomads. Most people live in large cities with modern facilities. Children go to free schools; there is free health care. Because of its oil and its role as the guardian of the holiest shrines of the Islamic religion, Saudi Arabia is an important part of two very different worlds: the traditional world of the Arab Islamic culture and the modern global world led by the industrialized nations of North America, Europe, and Japan.

The meeting of these two worlds in Saudi Arabia began less than 75 years ago, when oil was discovered in this Bedouin (nomadic Arab) kingdom. At the time, Saudi Arabia was one of the most remote and underdeveloped parts of the world. Since then, the country has been the scene of tremendous change. It has also been a site of conflict between traditional tribal and religious values symbolized by the Bedouin Arab and the modern world imported to the country because of the importance of Saudi oil.

THE FAMILY THAT RULES

Saudi Arabia's struggle between traditional ways and the modern lifestyle came with the search for oil. The country's name, Saudi Arabia, comes from the name of the Saud family. Abdul Aziz Al Saud, or Ibn Saud, a desert chieftain, created the country by uniting many local tribes in 1932, before oil was discovered. The Saud family has ruled the country ever since. The country has no congress or parliament, no supreme court, no president, and no elections. Since the adoption of the Basic Law in 1992, Saudi Arabia has been a monarchy whose rulers can come only from among the descendants of Ibn Saud.

The king and his family control the whole country as well as the vast pool of oil and natural gas under it. They own the company that produces the oil; they receive payment for all the oil that is exported, and they decide how to spend that money—for themselves, for their country, or for religious causes.

CENTER OF THE MUSLIM WORLD

Saudi Arabia is the center of Islam, one of the world's great religions. Today, there are more than 1.3 billion Muslims, the name given to those who follow Islam, in the world. Muslims form the majority of the population in 45 countries that extend from Indonesia in southeastern Asia westward to Morocco, on the Atlantic coast of North Africa, and southward into Africa.

For all these people, Allah is the one God, and the Prophet Muhammad is God's last great prophet. The words that God spoke to the Prophet Muhammad are recorded in the *Qur'an* (*Koran*), the sacred book of Muslims throughout the world. The Prophet Muhammad lived in the northwestern part of what is now Saudi Arabia from about A.D. 570 to 632. The Koran was written in Arabic, the language of the Prophet Muhammad.

The Saudi Arabian cities of Mecca, where the Prophet Muhammad was born and lived, and Medina, the home of the first adherents of the Prophet Muhammad's teachings and the site where he is buried, are the two most sacred Muslim cities in the world. Every Muslim is expected to make a pilgrimage to Mecca once in his or her lifetime. Millions of Muslims travel to Mecca—and on to Medina—each year. The Saudi government must organize the facilities used by those pilgrims and guide them through their holy rituals. The House of Saud, as the ruling family is called, sees its Islamic heritage as a sacred trust that makes Saudi Arabia especially important to Muslims throughout the world.

HOMELAND OF ARAB CULTURE

Arab culture, as identified with the Arabic language, has its roots in the Arabian Peninsula. That culture extends across North Africa from Morocco on the Atlantic coast to Egypt on the Red Sea. It reaches the heart of the Middle East in Jordan, Lebanon, Syria, and Iraq. In this area, 270 million people are called Arabs, speak the Arabic language, and are Muslims.

A Kingdom of Bedouin Tribes

At the core of Arab culture are the nomadic Bedouin tribes that, for thousands of years, herded camels, sheep, and goats on the desert fringes of the Arab world. These Bedouins were honored in Arab stories and myths, like the cowboys of America's heritage. Saudi Arabia is home to the most honored Bedouins, the camel herders. Like the Indian tribes of North America, the Bedouins lived in separate tribes in the deserts of the Middle East and North Africa. Arabia was made up of separate Bedouin tribes until Ibn Saud brought them all together to form Saudi Arabia.

Saudis: Conservative and Traditional

Saudi Arabia is one of the strictest Muslim countries. Oil has brought wealth to the Saudis, but they remain very conservative and cling tightly to their Bedouin culture and religious values. As part of the Bedouin tradition, the Saudis are faithful members of the Wahhabi sect of Islam (which falls under the Sunni school of Islam). It is one of the most fundamental and traditional of all sects. For the Saudis, there is no separation of church and state. The king and the House of Saud are believed to be carrying out God's law—*Sharia*, also known as Islamic law—as interpreted by Wahhabi religious leaders. As the Saud family modernizes their lives and their country, they must always consider what the new changes will mean to their Islamic faith. They feel that they must be very careful not to destroy traditional Muslim values.

Islamic principles and the working of the Saudi Arabian society revolve around the Sharia. Sharia means "the way" or "path to water" in Arabic. The teachings of Sharia are derived from four principal Islamic teachings. The most important source of Islamic law is the Koran, followed by the *hadith*, or record of the Prophet Muhammad's life, which is meant to be followed by all Muslims. The third most important source is *ijma*, or the consensus of Islamic scholars. The words of ijma are considered to be the law, and the king regularly consults ijma for his important decisions and for spiritual counseling.

The fourth most important source of the Sharia is *qiyas*, rules that forbid consumption of certain substances, including narcotics and prohibition of drinking alcoholic beverages.

Commercial and business transactions also are based on Sharia law. The system is divided into two divisions to govern Saudi society. On one hand, Sharia regulates the conduct of Islamic worship; on the other, it regulates human interactions, including marriage, law, and the legal system. Even eating habits that include avoidance of pork and alcohol is based on this law. In fact, the Koran specifically mentions that hogs are unclean and pork consumption should be avoided. Despite its Islamic roots, under Sharia, the judicial system shares some similarities with that of the United States. For example, in the U.S. legal system, all people are equal under the law and a person is considered innocent until proven guilty. This is the same in the Saudi legal system. The penalty for violating Sharia, however, is much more severe and in most cases can lead to capital punishment (death).

THE GLOBAL IMPORTANCE OF OIL

In the 1930s, geologists from U.S. oil companies (the Standard Oil Company of California and Texaco) discovered oil in the northeastern part of Saudi Arabia. Since then, scientists have estimated that oceans of oil lie under Saudi Arabia. Today, after more than half a century as the world's leading exporter of petroleum, about one-quarter of all the oil still known to be in the ground, as well as vast quantities of natural gas, remain under the surface of the country. Saudi Arabia has become a very important part of the modern world. Its influence on the oil industry is so great that a change in the Saud family's policies affects global energy consumption. For example, this was evident during the Yom Kippur War (between Israel and Egypt, Syria, Jordan, and Iraq) in 1973, when Saudi Arabia led the Arab nations in drastically cutting oil output to the West. This severely affected the industrial growth worldwide and inflicted a heavy blow to the U.S. economy.

Saudi Arabia is the world's largest producer of oil and holds approximately 25 percent of the world's proven oil reserves. Founded in the 1990s, the Shaybah oil field is one of Saudi Arabia's newest oil-producing regions and churns out half a million barrels of crude oil each day. Pictured here is a refinery that strips natural gas from the freshly pumped crude oil of the Shaybah region.

Oil accounts for about 40 percent of all the primary energy used in the world, and more than half of that energy is used by the United States, Canada, Japan, and countries of Europe. Japan has no oil production and most European countries have little, if any. The United States, the world's largest energy user, has oil, but still depends on foreign sources for almost two-thirds of its petroleum needs. Almost all of the oil that Saudi Arabia produces is exported to supply modern development throughout the world. The nation is not only the world's largest oil exporter, but it also possesses the largest amount of proven oil reserves—about one-fourth of the known remaining supply.

THE DIFFICULT TASK OF MODERNIZING

The modernization of Saudi Arabia has required a very difficult balancing of old values with new technology. Masses of non-Muslim technicians are needed to operate the oil fields, and to build roads, airports, hospitals, schools, and modern cities. Since the Persian Gulf War of 1991, there have even been U.S. military bases established in Saudi Arabia. Wahhabi fundamentalists believe all these changes pose a threat to the Islamic faith. In 1996, a bomb killed 19 Americans at a military base in Saudi Arabia. Among the country's religious extremists is terrorist leader Osama bin Laden, son of a wealthy Saudi merchant. Most of the terrorists who attacked the World Trade Center in New York City and the Pentagon in Washington, D.C., on September 11, 2001, were of Saudi origin. Bin Laden and his followers have declared a holy war against the United States and have demanded that U.S. military forces be removed from Saudi Arabian soil. This holy war also is being waged against the House of Saud and its efforts to change the country.

The conflict between old and new is one that takes place on the streets of Saudi cities and towns every day. It shows up very clearly in the treatment of women. In Saudi Arabia—and much of the rest of the Muslim world—women are heavily veiled and wear flowing robes when they leave their homes, so they will not attract the attention of men from outside their families. Women cannot pray in the same room as men. They must be chaperoned when they shop or travel. They are not even allowed to drive.

All this may sound like an attempt to punish women. To Saudi Muslims, however, it is simply part of their Wahhabi religious beliefs. For them, women are the heart of the family. As such, they must be protected. Wahhabis prefer that men dress in the flowing robes and the headscarves of Bedouins. They fear the corruption of outside influences. The country has no movie theaters, and the government controls television programs to protect the people from corrupting influences.

Saudis pray five times a day, facing the holy city of Mecca. In Saudi cities and towns, shops close their doors at prayer time. Whenever possible, people go to a mosque (Muslim religious building) for prayer.

With these restrictions, one can imagine the problems Wahhabis have with foreigners. Many people from other lands and cultures have come to work in the oil industry, or on one of the many projects the Saud family has begun to modernize the country. The Wahhabis want these foreigners— with their very different ways—to live in their own communities, away from the Saudi people. When the foreigners leave their compounds, the Wahhabis expect them to obey traditional Saudi rules. If they do not, religious police enforce those rules.

THE TEMPTATIONS AND DANGERS OF MONEY

Thanks to the billions of dollars that have been made through Saudi oil, the Saud ruling family—with 5,000 or more members— is now probably the richest in the world. They have spent money on homes in London, New York, Hollywood, and many other fashionable and costly urban centers. They also have splurged on ski lodges, villas, and luxury apartments in some of the world's most costly and exclusive resorts. They travel in luxury cars and private jets.

They have also spent billions of dollars on a series of five-year plans to develop their country. They have tapped new water sources and developed irrigation works; roads, airports, and new industries have been built; even new cities have risen in the desert. The Saud family has also given loans to other Islamic countries.

Saudi oil is not only important to the countries and companies of the modern world. It is also tempting to Saudi Arabia's larger neighbors, Iraq and Iran. Saudi money has gone into building a modern military equipped with jet aircraft, missiles, and tanks. To protect itself further, the Saudi government has signed treaties with the United States. The Saudis gain support from the world's greatest military power, and the United States receives a constant supply of Saudi Arabian oil.

During the past 50 years, Saudi Arabia has changed from a nation of poor tribal nomads to one of the richest countries in the world. During that time, the country has had to face countless difficult decisions. The major question has been: how to modernize while maintaining traditional Arab values. Trying to find the answers has put a severe strain on the country's rulers and its people that continues today.

OLD AND NEW AS SEEN FROM THE AIR

Flying on a commercial Saudi Arabian Airlines jet, the national carrier, the contrast between old and new ways becomes evident. In the plane, on one of the in-seat stereo channels, the Koran is recited continuously. Passengers include Arabs dressed in fine, tailor-made suits and others wearing the traditional red-and-white Arab headdress and flowing robe. Some women wear the latest fashions, while others wear traditional robes and veils. In the rear of the plane is an area where Muslims can spread their prayer rugs. An electronic arrow points in the direction of Mecca.

As the plane approaches Jiddah, the busiest airport in the country, some of the basic aspects of the country can be seen from the window. There is no question that this is a desert world. The land below is brown and gray, with barren upland ridges poking out. In the midst of this dry world, close to the city there are patches of green fields and rows of planted date palms, part of the newly created irrigated land. Jiddah, itself, is a sprawl of white and beige. The city center has a few modern high-rises, and much of the rest of the city contains closely packed apartment buildings 3 to 10 stories high. From the modern airport extends a network of four-lane highways.

As the plane taxies to the modern terminal, high-rise hotels can be seen. The roads are crowded with cars and trucks. In one area of the field, the private jets of the Saud family can taxi up to the door of one of their mansions right at the airport.

In another corner of the airport, however, a gigantic tent covers several acres. There, people in traditional robes and veils are cooking over open fires, sleeping on mats on the floor, drinking coffee, and talking. Children run and play, dodging goats, donkeys, and camels. These are Bedouin Muslim pilgrims on their way to Mecca. They did not come on airplanes or ships; they walked or rode on camels, as their ancestors have done for centuries.

CHAPTER

2

Physical Landscapes

Although it is part of Asia, Saudi Arabia actually occupies most of the large Arabian Peninsula that separates Africa from mainland Asia. To the west and south, the narrow Red Sea and the Gulf of Aden divide the Arabian Peninsula from Africa. To the east, the Persian Gulf and Gulf of Oman lie between the peninsula and Asia proper. The southeastern portion of the peninsula faces the part of the Indian Ocean known as the Arabian Sea.

THE ARABIAN PENINSULA

Saudi Arabia makes up most of the Arabian Peninsula. The small countries of Kuwait, Bahrain, Qatar, and the United Arab Emirates lie along the Persian Gulf in the east. The country of Oman is located on the southeastern part of the peninsula, between the Gulf of Oman and the Arabian Sea. Yemen occupies most of the southern coast along the Arabian Sea.

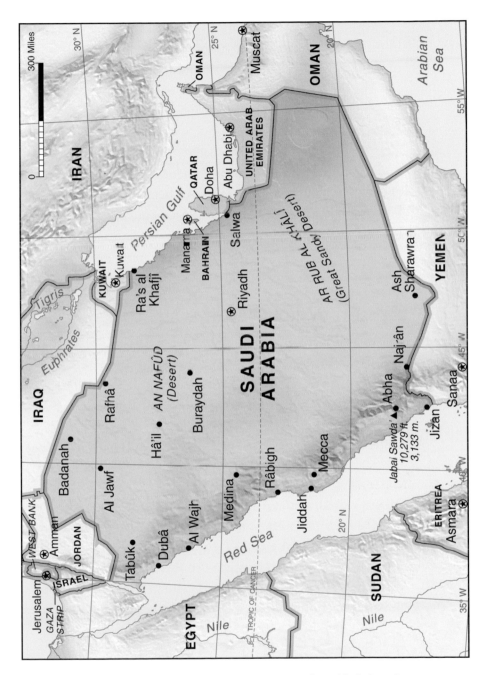

Primarily made up of parched desert landscape, Saudi Arabia is largely uninhabited, and less than 2 percent of its land is arable, or able to sustain crops. Saudi Arabia's highest point, Jabal Sawda' (10,279 feet, 3,133 meters), is located in the southwestern part of the country, near the Red Sea and Yemen.

On the world geopolitical map, Saudi Arabia is quite impressive. It is the largest country in the Middle East and is much larger than any European country, except Russia.

The world population map, however, tells another story. Most of Saudi Arabia has few, if any, people. In fact, a large area of the country is known as the "Empty Quarter." Although the capital city, Riyadh, is in the country's interior, most Saudis live close to the coasts of the Red Sea and the Persian Gulf. In all, there are only about 27 million people in Saudi Arabia, approximately 5 million more than the population of Texas, which is only one-third the size of Saudi Arabia. Each of Saudi Arabia's Middle Eastern neighbors—Iran, Egypt, and Turkey—has more than 65 million people, nearly two and a half times the Saudi population.

A DESERT SURROUNDED BY SEAS

Even though Saudi Arabia is surrounded by water on two sides, it is primarily a parched desert landscape. Less than 1 percent of Saudi Arabia is forested, and only 1 percent of its land is farmed. (1 percent of the country is an area about the size of Massachusetts within an area approximately the size of the United States, east of the Mississippi River.)

The country is located near the center of the world's largest belt of dry climate. Arid conditions extend across North Africa's Sahara Desert, to the Arabian Peninsula, and into Afghanistan and Pakistan in south Asia. In central Asia, the bone-dry arid landscape reaches the Gobi Desert that occupies much of the western half of China. Nearly all of this huge area receives less than 10 inches (25 centimeters) of rainfall a year, less than one-fourth the amount most of the eastern United States receives. The arid climate is caused by a huge high-pressure system in the atmosphere that lies over the area most of the year. High pressure is associated with clear, dry weather and rarely produces precipitation.

The Arabian Peninsula is separated from Africa and the Asian mainland by geological forces. The earth consists of a series of plates, separated by deep cracks that formed as the earth cooled over billions of years. Each continent sits on a separate plate, or plates. The Arabian Peninsula is separated from the main mass of the Eurasian Plate by a break that is filled by the Persian Gulf. There, the crack between the plates is slowly widening.

West of the peninsula, the Red Sea was formed by a crack in Earth's crust at the edge of a plate. This crack, called a rift, is the longest single break that can be traced over Earth's land surface—more than 3,000 miles (4,828 kilometers). Its northern end forms the trench occupied by the Jordan River that flows between Israel and Jordan into the Dead Sea. The shore of this extremely salty water body is 1,371 feet (418 meters) below sea level, making it the lowest elevation (of dry land) on Earth's surface. The rift then extends southward to form the Gulf of Aqaba, an arm of the Red Sea, and the long, narrow trench occupied by the Red Sea itself. Finally, the rift continues southward across eastern Africa, where it crosses Ethiopia and Kenya, before it finally disappears into Mozambique.

Some of the oldest rock in the world is exposed in the western part of the Arabian Peninsula. It is very hard, having been changed by heat and pressure from deep within the earth over billions of years.

Uplands separate the Arabian Peninsula from Israel and Jordan in the northwest and from Iraq in the north. Mountains form an almost continuous ridge along the peninsula's western coast. Mountains are also present along the southeastern coast of Yemen, and border the southern part of the Red Sea and the Gulf of Aden. Here are found the highest mountains on the peninsula, rising just over 12,000 feet (3,658 meters). The tallest peak in Saudi Arabia is 10,279-foot-high (3,133-meter-high) Jabal Sawda', located about 100 miles (161 kilometers) southeast of Mecca.

The peninsula is like a giant basin that drops away from high mountain ridges along the Red Sea coast to the low-lying shore of the Persian Gulf. In the middle of this great basin, in the center of the Arabian Peninsula, there are several long, low ridges that arc for hundreds of miles across the almost barren desert landscape.

PHYSICAL REGIONS

Geographers point out five physical subregions in Saudi Arabia. They are the rugged west, the rocky interior, the low-lying plains of the east, the northern border uplands, and the "Empty Quarter" of the south. In the west, mountains stretch from Yemen and the Gulf of Aden northward to the Gulf of Aqaba and the border with Jordan. The continuous ridge forms the eastern wall of the Rift Valley that is filled by the water of the Red Sea. There are only a few scattered narrow coastal plains along the shore of the sea. Because it is formed by a huge geological fault, the shoreline of the Red Sea is quite straight, and has few good harbors. The Saudis divide the long ridge into two regions, based on important differences.

The Hejaz (The Northwest)

There are very few easy routes through the mountainous ridge between the coast and the interior. Because of the terrain and the difficulty of travel, the region is called the *Hejaz* (the barrier). The western mountains are not very high. Some peaks reach above 8,000 feet (2,438 meters), but most of the ridges average about 5,000 feet (1,524 meters) in elevation. The region derives its name, "the barrier," not only because the mountain ridge is an almost continuous chain, but because it is tilted so that the western walls, along the Red Sea, are very steep. This has made it difficult for outsiders to enter the Arabian Peninsula from the west. The eastern slopes are much gentler than those of the west. They form the upper part of the basin that extends across the Arabian Peninsula.

Short *wadis* (stream courses that are dry most of the year, but may carry torrents of water after a rain) have formed deep gorges, or gaps, in the steep western wall of the ridges, but few

The Hejaz, which means "barrier" in Arabic, is a province in northwestern Saudi Arabia. Here, al-Noor Mountain serves as a backdrop for one of the Muslim world's holiest cities, Mecca, which also serves as the capital of the Hejaz.

of the gorges pass entirely through the ridge. One gap extends inland eastward from coastal Jiddah to Mecca, then northeastward to Medina, in the interior of the basin. Jiddah, Mecca, and Medina are ancient cities located along trade routes that made use of the mountain gap.

Historically, the Hejaz has been one of the most important regions of the Arabian Peninsula. Trade routes between the eastern Mediterranean Sea and Yemen and the Arabian Sea to the south followed the eastern edge of the uplands. Over time, the people from this part of Arabia have had more contact with the rest of the world than have most other Arabians.

Azir (The Southwest)

South of the Jiddah-Mecca gap, small but important changes occur along the Red Sea. The mountains rise higher, but a narrow coastal plan has formed, making land travel easier. There, the climate is more subtropical. In the extreme southwest, near the border with Yemen, the ridge along the Red Sea joins the mountains of the southwest coast of the Arabian Sea. Here, a number of peaks reach more than 9,000 feet (2,743 meters), with the highest towering just over 12,000 feet (3,658 meters). One result of this region's higher elevation is that more rain falls here than in the Hejaz, or anywhere else on the peninsula. In fact, there is enough rainfall here to support the peninsula's only forests. Here, too, the valleys have long been farmed and the lower hills used for grazing livestock.

The most intensively settled area is along the narrow coastal strip called the Tihama. Along the Red Sea shore, the plain is salty from the tides. The rest of the lowland, however, has fertile alluvial soil washed from the mountains by rains and deposited on the flat plain. Good soil and adequate moisture are not the only advantages of this agricultural area. It is also the area of Saudi Arabia closest to the equator. This combination of soil and warm temperatures allow farmers to produce tropical crops. The potential for growing specialty crops is so important that many of the mountain slopes have been terraced in order to create more land to farm. Many Arabs consider this area to have been the site of the Bible's Garden of Eden.

In Azir, the eastern mountain slopes are gentle. A number of wadis and rich alluvial soils have combined to create fertile oasis sites that are excellent for farming. Coffee has long been an important crop of the region.

For thousands of years, the nomadic Bedouin tribes of Saudi Arabia have herded many varieties of animals, including camels. Most of Saudi Arabia's Bedouins live in the parched uplands of the Nadj, which is located east of the Hejaz, in the country's interior.

The Nadj (The Interior)

East of the Hejaz and Azir is a parched, mostly rocky upland formed of ancient crystalline rock. Parts of the region are covered with small sandy deserts and a few clumps of mountains, but rock covers much of the surface.

About halfway across the peninsula, two deeply eroded, relatively low, northwest-southeast trending ridges form an S-shaped barrier that crosses almost the entire country. Like the Hejaz wall, these ridges have steep west-facing slopes and much gentler eastern slopes. However, the ridges rise only a few hundred feet above the plateau, and there are gaps throughout them. The longest, highest ridge, called Jabal Tuwayq, is the source of water for a number of oasis towns.

West of the ridges lies the higher Upper Nadj. Here, there are no sedimentary rocks that might hold oil. A few long wadi valleys in the gentle slopes of the western mountains carry water that flows only briefly after an occasional rain. Some streams disappear into the dry ground, and then reappear farther east. Even though the wadis are usually dry, when the water flows, much of it seeps into the ground. Wells are dug to reach this moisture, and provide water to oasis sites throughout the year. Most villages and towns in this very dry region are found near the wadis.

Protected by the mountainous Hadj in the west, the Nadj is surrounded by a different sort of barrier to the north, east, and south. There, a great arc of deserts makes travel very difficult. To the north, the Great Nafud (*nafud* means "desert") is covered with long sand dunes that are separated by valleys more than 15 miles (25 kilometers) wide. The sand gives the desert a reddish hue. There are several watering places, and scant winter rains bring short-lived grasses on which Bedouin herds graze.

East of the central oases that include Riyadh is the Ad Dahna, a narrow band of sand that extends for almost 800 miles (1,287 kilometers). This area separates the heart of the Nadj from the coastal areas of the Persian Gulf. It is called "the river of sand." Winds keep the sand continually moving as in a slow-flowing stream, and there are few watering places.

The Nadj is the heartland of Arabian Bedouin culture and the home of the House of Saud. Throughout history, it was occupied by many camel-herding Bedouin tribes and by some of Arabia's most important oasis towns and villages. The Saud family is from the area along the west side of the Jabal Tuwayq.

Their most dangerous enemies lived in the large oasis of Ha'il, located in the Jabal Shammar Mountains, between Riyadh and the northern desert.

Al-Hasa (The Northeast)

East of the interior slopes, the land is lower. It gently drops to the low-lying shores of the Persian Gulf. Here, the ancient crystalline rocks of the west are buried deep below sedimentary rock. It is these layers of sedimentary rock that hold vast deposits of oil. Much of the surface itself is covered with sand. Before the discovery of oil, this was a sparsely populated region, except along the coast of the Persian Gulf. The Saudis call the region *Al-Hasa*. The name comes from a great oasis located here, the largest in the entire country.

Between the Ad Dahna and the Nadj is a barren, rocky upland about 70 miles (113 kilometers) wide. To the east, however, the coastal area along the Persian Gulf is mostly low-lying, rolling plain covered with a thin layer of sand and gravel. Bushes and sparse grass hold the sand in low dunes, called hummocks, that give the land a bumpy character. The southern half of the Saudi coast is another belt of high, windblown dunes.

Al-Hasa and the Persian Gulf

This lowland extends into Kuwait in the north and continues in the south through Bahrain and the United Arab Emirates. Boundaries between these countries are just imaginary lines drawn in the sand. Bedouins have long moved across them. Saudi Arabia and Kuwait have agreed on a "neutral zone" between them, where the countries share development and oil revenues. The continuation of the coastal lowland north into Kuwait and Iraq make the Saudi borders with these countries the most vulnerable to attack.

The Persian Gulf is shallow, and its water is dotted with offshore sandbars and coral reefs. As a result, there are no good natural harbors, although there are many small inlets that, throughout history, have provided shelter for *dhows* (small sailing boats). Only by building very long docks to reach deeper water can oil tankers be loaded at some Persian Gulf ports.

The sedimentary rock holds the vast pool of oil that has made Saudi Arabia so important to the global economy. The oil is great in quantity, is found close to the surface, is of high quality, and is close to the sea for easy export. Oil flows from many wells without pumping. As a result, petroleum can be produced much more cheaply than in most of the world's other oil fields. Oil has completely changed this region. In addition to the many oil wells, storage tanks, and pipelines, new deepwater ports and cities to house oil workers have been built. A large percentage of the residents of this region are foreign workers.

Northern Arabia

The Arabian basin also has a northern edge. Here, a high upland extends from the border with Jordan and western Iraq. It rises to a height of 2,900 feet (884 meters) and forms a drainage divide. To the east, waters flow into the Euphrates River system, once home to the great civilizations of Mesopotamia and Assyria, and today the heartland of Iraq. The uplands are covered with desert grass and scrub vegetation, and nomadic herders use them as pastures.

West of the divide is a depression 200 miles (322 kilometers) long, 20 to 30 miles (32 to 48 kilometers) wide, and 1,000 feet (305 meters) below the surrounding countryside. This basin is known as Wadi as Sirhan. Like the rift, it was created by shifting rocks.

The northern region gives way to the Great Nafud at its southern edge. The combination of rugged upland terrain and desert sands has discouraged settlement in the north. This empty desert does, however, form a good defensive zone against possible invasion from Saudi Arabia's northern Middle Eastern neighbors.

Located in southeastern Saudi Arabia, the Ar Rub al-Khali, or Empty Quarter, is the largest area of continuous sand in the world. The region is 250,000 square miles (650,000 square kilometers) and covers approximately a quarter of Saudi Arabia. Here, a massive sand dune rises above cracked salt flats in the Ar Rub al-Khali.

Ar Rub al-Khali (The Empty Quarter)

The vast sandy areas east of the interior slopes of the Nadj sweep southward into southern Saudi Arabia. The south is known as the Rub al-Khali, the vast "Empty Quarter." This huge sea of sand, the world's largest, stretches for about 750 miles (1,207 kilometers) across the entire southern part of the country. It is nearly 400 miles (644 kilometers) wide where it merges with sandy areas farther north. The sand covers an area about the size of Texas, or Canada's Alberta province. Some areas are covered with sand sheets, but there are also sand dunes that constantly shift with the howling desert winds. The winds fashion dunes into many interesting shapes, including mountainous ridges of sand 500 to 800 feet (150 to 250 meters) high.

The Empty Quarter is well named. It is so dry that there are few places where even camels or goats can graze. It was one of the last parts of the world to be explored by Western-ers. It was not until the early 1930s that the first European explorers ventured into this hostile region. And it was the last place on Earth (other than Antarctica) to be divided by political boundaries.

EVER-PRESENT DRYNESS

The most obvious physical feature of Saudi Arabia is its dry climate. The country's aridity has produced the rugged ter-rain of the uplands and the vast sandy areas in the lowland. The landforms have been shaped by windblown sand and the erosive force of torrents of water following the few rains, as is common in desert areas. It does not rain often, but when it does, rain usually comes in the form of heavy downpours. There is almost no vegetation to slow the water as it runs off the desert slopes. Stream valleys that are normally dry become raging watercourses that tear away the land and move heavy boulders. These are the wadis. They pose the threat of destruc-tive flash floods, but they also offer excellent sources of well water, which is important since Saudi Arabia has no perma-nently flowing rivers.

True Desert

Most of Saudi Arabia is true desert, receiving only 3 to 4 inches (7 to 10 centimeters) of precipitation a year. Significant rain occurs only in the mountains of the southwest, where as much as 20 inches (51 centimeters) may fall during a normal year.

No region has a traditional rainy season. A bit more rain falls along the east coast during the winter, the result of moisture being carried by winds from the Mediterranean Sea. An isolated storm can occur at any time, but thundershowers, particularly in mountainous areas, are more frequent in summer months. Rainfall consists of one or two heavy downpours a year. Wadis flood, then the water disappears rapidly into the earth. Many parts of the country may go several years without rain. In the Empty Quarter, in fact, an entire decade can pass without rain.

Windstorms often occur in June and July. Blowing over the vast areas of dry ground and sand, winds of 25 to 30 miles (40 to 48 kilometers) an hour, with gusts up to 65 miles (105 kilometers) an hour, can blow sand particles three feet or more into the air. Dust rises hundreds of feet. Like a snow blizzard in the U.S. or Canadian Great Plains, sandstorms may make visibility impossible and may last for several days. It is winds of this kind that shape the rock outcroppings and keep sand dunes moving.

Less-Dry Areas

Although the Tropic of Cancer, at 23½° north latitude, cuts directly across the center of Saudi Arabia, the only area that has anything approaching a humid tropical climate is the narrow coastal lowland of the Asiz, near Yemen. There, monsoon winds that blow water over the land produce most of the yearly rainfall between October and March.

The coastal lowland along the Persian Gulf north of the Tropic of Cancer has the feel of the humid tropics because of its high summer humidity, even though there is little rainfall. Such humidity often produces fog and dew—a substitute for rainfall. In most of the rest of the country, the humidity is almost always extremely low.

TEMPERATURE EXTREMES

Low humidity and mostly cloudless skies produce great extremes of temperature, from season to season and even from day to night, in the interior. Under the blazing summer sun, official temperatures can reach 130°F (54°C), but much higher in the direct sunlight. It is extremely hot from dawn to dusk, but at night temperatures may fall almost as low as 60°F (16°C). Because Arabia is on the fringe of the tropics, winters would not be expected to be long or cold, but at night temperatures in the northern half of the country can drop below freezing. Snow sometimes falls in northern Saudi Arabia, particularly in the mountains. It has even snowed in Riyadh, which lies deep in the interior of the country.

In such a dry country, much of the land is barren of vegetation. The vast areas of sand have virtually no plant life. In some places, a few deep-rooted shrubs with few leaves have adapted to the desert conditions. Many small flowering plants, dormant most of the time, spring into life and bloom during the few days after the infrequent rains.

THE IMPORTANCE OF WATER

In much of Saudi Arabia today, as in the past, the limiting factor for human life, as well as other animals and plants, has been the availability of water. Until oil production and modern technology came along, permanent settlements were located only at the few places with a reliable source of water on or near the surface. That pattern of settlement is gradually changing.

3

Life in the Desert

Throughout recorded history, most inhabitants of the Arabian Peninsula have been Bedouins (the word means "desert dweller"), who were skilled in utilizing the sparse desert water sources. To live, they have depended on animals—mostly camels and goats, but horses as well—that could survive under desert conditions. When they see the lightning of a desert storm, Bedouins move their herds and flocks toward it to take advantage of the small plants that grow for a few weeks after a storm. When there is no rain, they congregate around wells. In periods of drought, one Bedouin tribe might move onto land occupied by another tribe. There have often been fierce battles over grazing lands or wells.

THE BEDOUINS

The term *Bedouin* is used differently by various people. Not all Bedouins were nomadic herders. City people refer to all villagers as Bedouins. There have always been close ties between the desert herders and villagers. Each has products the other wants. The camels, sheep, and horses of the Bedouins are highly prized in villages, and the nomads want the grain, dates, utensils, and other supplies they could get from villagers. In the past, nomadic Bedouins who engaged in camel trading or other trade might settle a branch of their family in an oasis. In fact, the Saud family, often considered Bedouins, was made up of villagers, rather than nomadic herders.

Desert Life

Desert life produced a code of behavior. Since a traveler would die without water, the code says that any visitor—even an enemy—will be offered hospitality in a Bedouin camp for three days. After all, in the future, the Bedouins themselves might need the hospitality of others.

In a Bedouin community, men look after the animal herds and decide what moves the tribe will make. The tribe is led by a sheik, but his authority depends on the consent of the other tribesmen. Women are responsible for domestic duties—finding fuel, hauling water, doing the cooking, raising the children, and even packing and unpacking tents during a move.

Camels: "Ships of the Desert"

Camels and goats are well suited to desert life. Both need very little water and will feed on thorny plants, the leaves and twigs of desert shrubs, and dried grasses that other animals refuse to eat.

The camels of Saudi Arabia are dromedaries, one-humped animals with short hair. They can live under desert conditions that are difficult even for goats. When the feeding is good, they store fat in their humps. This fat can sustain them when food is scarce. The fat not only supplies energy, but can be converted into water within the camel's cells. Camels have special internal mechanisms that are designed to make the best use of water. Their body temperature can rise as much as 6°F (3°C) before they begin to sweat and lose body moisture. A camel can drink

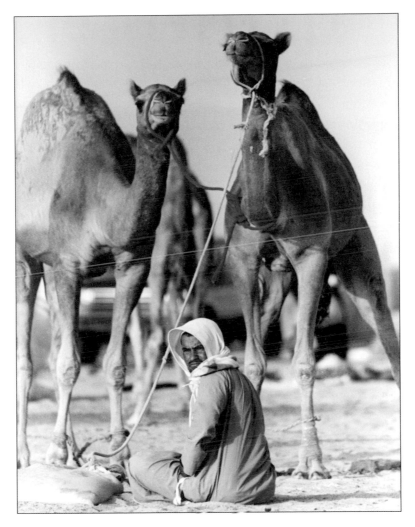

The one-humped dromedary camel was first domesticated on the southern Arabian Peninsula between three and six thousand years ago. Camels are traded throughout Saudi Arabia, because they are suited to the arid conditions—they can survive for up to two weeks without water and about a month without food.

water that is high in salts and minerals, and convert it to milk. Camels can even recycle their urine. Thus, they can go without eating or drinking for several days. During such periods, camels may lose up to a quarter of their weight by dehydration without ill effects. They can regain that lost weight in 10 minutes by drinking as much as 25 to 50 gallons (95 to 190 liters) of water.

At the height of summer, when the supply of food for grazing is poor, a camel may need to drink every four days, but in winter when the pasture is good, a camel may go several weeks between drinks. During the winter, Bedouins do not worry about watering their camels.

Dromedaries are protected from desert sand. They have double rows of heavy eyelashes and hairy ear openings to protect them in sandstorms. They can even close their nostrils. They have a keen sense of sight and smell. With their short hair, they withstand extreme heat well. They even have large, soft, padded feet that work like snowshoes, allowing them to walk over drift sand without sinking. The camel's long neck allows it to nibble low-lying desert plants and also eat leaves from trees. The neck also gives the animal balance as it runs.

Before four-wheel-drive trucks and SUVs, camels were the freight-carrying "ships of the desert." Caravans of dozens of camels carried goods across Arabia between the Persian Gulf and the Mediterranean coast, to avoid the long sea voyage around Arabia and the length of the Red Sea. A single camel can easily carry more than 400 pounds (181 kilograms). With their low water and food needs, camels were very cheap to use in the desert. A camel caravan could travel where horse- or ox-driven vehicles could not go.

Nomads who depended primarily on camels raised herds of 100 or more. The camels were not usually raised for food. Sheep and goats provided the Bedouin meat supply. Male camels were used as baggage carriers when the nomads moved, but most camels were sold in market towns along the caravan routes that skirted the desert edge. In return for their camels, the Bedouins received the dates, rice, bread, coffee and tea, and sheep and goats that made up their basic diet. Camel sales also allowed the nomads to buy clothing, tools, weapons, and even the goat hair used for their black tents. The replacement of camel caravans by trucks and roads forced many Bedouins to move to towns. There was no longer a market for their camels. Female camels were kept for breeding, and especially for their milk, which was an important part of the Bedouin diet.

Famous Horses

The Arabian Peninsula is also home to Arabian horses, famous for their intelligence, grace, and speed. Mounted on camels and these horses, the Bedouins raided oasis towns and settlements. Later, these raiders led the Islamic conquest of the Middle East and North Africa. Today, the Arabian horse is highly prized throughout the world. The racing stables of the Saud family are among the world's most famous. Races are held in Riyadh each year.

Shepherds

Camel Bedouins live in the drier parts of the desert. Closer to the desert fringe, where better pastures are found, the Bedouins are sheepherders. Their life is similar to that of camel herders. Sheepherders move their flocks from place to place, seeking pasture and water. Today, it is more profitable to raise sheep than camels. Both meat and wool can be sold in town markets. Sheep also reproduce more rapidly, and provide milk and wool for the Bedouins' own use. As vehicles replaced camels, some camel Bedouins shifted to sheep herding. However, like cattlemen in the American West, camel Bedouins have always considered sheepherders to be at a lower social level.

Bedouins Face Modern Life

As Saudi Arabia has moved into the modern world as a result of oil production and the development of cities, Bedouin life has changed. The Saudi government has tried hard to move the nomads into cities. Housing has been built for them, and they have been given taxis and trucks so they can do city work, as well as education to prepare them for city jobs. Many have adopted city life, but it has been hard. Some have tried to keep the best of both worlds, moving their tents, herds, and flocks to the edge of cities. Often, the males of the family will take city jobs, leaving the women to care for the animals and the family.

Traditional Saudi Dress

Saudi dress is very well adapted to hot desert conditions. Men wear *aghai*, a double headcord worn over the *ghutra*, a flowing headdress (red-and-white-checkered in winter, white in summer); *mislah*, a flowing outer robe; and *thobe*, a full-length white, thin, skirtlike garment worn under the robe. Women wear scarves or woven head wraps that cover every strand of hair; veils; long petticoats under floor-length dresses with long sleeves and high necks; and *abaya*, a long black cloak.

Changes in Bedouin Life and Culture

Some Bedouins still cling to nomadic life. Even for these people, many changes have occurred. Pickup trucks now transport the Bedouins from place to place. The nomads have gas-fired cook stoves and modern weapons, but they continue to live in tents. The number of camels a family owns continues to be a measure of wealth. Bedouins who now live in cities still invest in livestock, which are herded by members of their family who practice a nomadic lifestyle.

Over centuries, the Bedouins became skilled at knowing where a temporary water source and a bit of grazing land could be found at different times of the year. They learned the seasonal patterns of rainfall, changing their pattern of movement from year to year as the rains varied. They developed a system of movement, moving from wadi to wadi, well to well, sometimes spending as much as a month at a given water source before moving on to another. Their life was dependent on the desert animals that provided meat, milk, and hides for clothing and tents, even dried dung for fuel.

Even though only a small number of Saudis today still follow the nomadic lifestyle, Saudis are proud of their Bedouin heritage. The Saudi image of a real Arab is the Bedouin. The Bedouin is tough and resourceful; he practices true, traditional Wahhabi religion; and he is a savage fighter. Most of all, he is independent and free.

WATER: KEY TO SURVIVAL IN AN ARID LAND

Water is essential to all life. In arid lands it can severely limit where people live and what they do (or are unable to do), and how they do it. For Saudi Arabia, having an adequate supply of this precious resource is essential to the country's future. Before the discovery of oil, there was little crop agriculture in Arabia, except along the coastal plain of the Red Sea, in the nearby mountain valleys, and the scattered oases with reliable water sources. Date palms, in particular, can be grown in areas with very little water. Dates are a dietary staple for both the Bedouin and city dwellers alike. The only area with sufficient rainfall for nonirrigated farming is in the far southwestern region of the country on the western flank of the Asir Mountains. Because the mountains serve as a barrier to moisture-bearing winds along their windward flank, air is forced upward, cooled, and the resulting rainfall is sufficient to sustain dry-land farming (farming in a semiarid region without irrigation).

Scarcity of water and irregular rainfall has been a recurring problem for Saudi farmers. From Ta'if in the north to Jizan in the south, this narrow agricultural belt has helped sustain Saudi Arabia for centuries. The coastal plains of Tihamah have also contributed to subsistence farming in recent years. Recent irrigation projects using water from springs and wells also has helped scattered agricultural developments in the Western Highlands. Toward the interior, especially at Najd, An Nafud,

Saudi Arabia is the world's second-largest producer of dates, behind Iran. A staple of the Bedouin diet, dates are a popular commodity at Saudi markets, such as the one pictured here in Riyadh, where two Saudi men sell their wares.

and in the vicinity of the nation's capital of Riyadh, availability of groundwater has helped farming develop.

Water Supply

The most widespread aquifers (groundwater resources) are found in the areas of heavier rainfall in the mountains near the Red Sea. However, there are a few aquifers under the bone-dry interior of Saudi Arabia, where water may have been stored since prehistoric times. Other aquifers are supplied by waters that have fallen in the coastal mountains hundreds of miles away from where they eventually pool. It has taken hundreds of years for the water to move that far. Most of the aquifers of the

interior are in pockets on either side of the S-shaped ridges that
extend across the center of the country. The capital, Riyadh, is
a city that was built over such an aquifer.

Modern deep-well pumps can deliver large quantities of
water daily, enough for city use and also for irrigated agriculture
in the middle of the desert. However, the aquifers are essentially
being mined. Like the oil in the rocks, the water that has been
in the ground all these years is being pumped out, and, like oil,
the supply is not being replenished. The result is that the "water
table"—the upper limit of the water in the aquifer—is being
drawn down, so that wells have to be drilled deeper and deeper.
At the present rate of use, these underground water reservoirs
will soon be completely used up.

For Saudi Arabia, the water issue is critical to economic
growth and is an even larger problem for the future. Oil
money has been used to find alternative water sources. The
most likely source is seawater from the water bodies that wash
the country's eastern and western shores. The ocean saltwater
is distilled in huge plants to produce freshwater. The process,
called *desalination*, is very expensive and uses huge amounts of
energy relative to the amount of water that is produced. The
water produced in this way is also flat and tasteless. In recent
years, however, desalination has attracted renewed interest.
Today, more than two-dozen desalination plants are actively
converting Red Sea and Persian Gulf water into clean drinking
water through advanced technologies. Presently, Saudi Arabia
is the largest exporter of desalinized water in the world. Engineers have even considered towing huge icebergs from Antarctica as a source of water for Saudi Arabia!

Water Law

Saudi Arabia's adherence to the Sharia Islamic law extends to its
water policies. According to Sharia and Islamic custom, utiliza-
tion of water follows a hierarchy of needs. Water is prescribed
to be used first for domestic purpose, followed by water for

animals, and finally water for agriculture. Thus, community interest and water for the welfare of Saudi citizens is a priority. The government has regulated water policies centered on the Sharia water laws, and accordingly, national water demands are regulated. Similar to permission required to drill oil fields, Sharia law administers regulations regarding well drilling from an aquifer. In a royal decree passed in 1980, regulative laws were introduced in protecting aquifers from massive exploitation and water pollution, thereby protecting the fragile groundwater system in the desert interior. Today, Saudi Arabia's Ministry of Water and Agriculture monitors this royal decree by issuing permits prior to drilling wells.

Wastewater Management

In recent years, Saudi Arabia has made great strides in recycling its wastewater as a new source of clean water. In 1978, a *fatwa* (legal judgment) was passed by the Council of Leading Islamic Scholars that initiated the process of recycling Saudi Arabia's wastewater. Fatwa is another important religious facet of the Saudi Arabian governance system. A fatwa is a declaration that is usually decided by Islamic scholars or intellectuals and is considered the rule of the land in several Islamic nations. Different degrees of treating wastewater exist today, with each water type serving different functions. For instance, in Jubail, an industrial city located on the eastern coast of the nation, the wastewater recycling process has increased over the years with recent growth in industrial and shipping activities. Recycled wastewater has helped drier interior regions, including the royal capital city, Riyadh, to sustain its plantations and other agriculture. Urban landscaping and development of parks have been made possible with recycled water as a valuable resource in other cities, including Jiddah, Taif, and Dhahran.

Growth in population and increase in agricultural activity has forced Saudi Arabia to focus on its future water resource with great attention. Water conservation and management is one of the key priorities of this arid region. Focused agricultural methods, including microirrigation and extensive use of sprinkler systems to increase farmland with minimal water, are some of these conservation techniques.

CHAPTER

4

People and Culture

The spatial distribution of Saudi Arabia's 27 million people is the result of many factors: the availability of water; the importance of Mecca and Medina as Muslim sites, and the importance of the port and airport of Jiddah; the center of government for the kingdom in Riyadh in the traditional Saud family homeland, east of the S-ridges in the interior of the country; the development of oil in the northeast, near the Persian Gulf; and the location of the one agricultural region in the coastal plain and nearby mountain valleys of the Azir.

WHERE THEY LIVE

Roughly one-third of the Saudi people live near the Red Sea, most of them in the cities of Jiddah, Mecca, and Medina. Another third of the people live in an area centered at Riyadh, on either side of the S-ridge in the interior. The final third live in the oil field region of the northeast, centered at the oil port of Ad Dammam.

Today, Bedouins account for only a tiny fraction of the population. Most Saudis—about 9 of every 10—live in cities. Riyadh has more than 4 million people, Jiddah at around 3.5 million, Mecca more than 1 million, and Medina more than 800,000. In the oil-producing area in the northeast, Ad Dammam is home to about 1.6 million people.

ARABS

Saudi Arabia takes its name from its people and its rulers. The native people are Arabs, who are a very ancient people, even though the nation of Saudi Arabia itself is less than 100 years old.

Arabs account for about two-thirds of the population of Saudi Arabia. However, Saudi Arabs are just one part of the much larger Arab ethnic group that makes up most of the population of Iraq, Syria, Lebanon, Jordan, Kuwait, and Egypt in the Middle East. The Palestinians in Israel, Jordan, and Lebanon are also Arabs, as are most of the people of North Africa in Libya, Tunisia, Algeria, Morocco, and Sudan.

Physically, Arabs are Semites (the race to which Jews also belong), who apparently first appeared on the Arabian Peninsula long before the beginnings of recorded history. One of the Arabs' roots can be traced to the southwestern portion of the Arabian Peninsula, where Yemen is now. The other comes from north-central Arabia. Tradition has it that Abraham, patriarch of the Bible's Old Testament, was of the second branch. Abraham had two sons: Isaac, by his wife, Sarah, became the patriarch of the Jewish people, and Ishmael, by his slave Hagar, became the patriarch of the Arabs.

Two Different Traditions

Middle Eastern Arabs can be separated into two traditions: those who became nomadic herders in the desert, and those who lived in towns and villages, chiefly as either farmers, tending gardens of date palms, or traders who bought wool,

Located in Mecca, the Ka'ba is Islam's holiest place. Many Muslims make the annual pilgrimage, or hajj, to Mecca during the month of Dhu al-Hijja, which marks the end of the Islamic year. Here, worshippers pray around the Ka'ba in the Masjid al-Haram during the hajj in 2003.

sheep, and camels from the nomads and sold them. People in the towns learned about life in the non-Arab world through their trade contacts. The nomads, or Bedouins, on the other hand, had little outside contact, even with the nearby villagers. Contact with villagers was often limited to the times when the Bedouins raided a village.

The ways of the Bedouins of Saudi Arabia were very different from the civilizations based on agriculture that developed in Mesopotamia (now Iraq) and of Egypt. Both of those cultures used the seasonal floods of rivers (the Tigris and Euphrates in Iraq, and Nile in Egypt) to irrigate crops that produced great wealth and supported large populations. Saudi Arabia has no such rivers. Tribes had to migrate from the desert to the wetter, fertile lands along the eastern Mediterranean Sea, as the nomadic tribes of the Old Testament had done.

As a result of these problems, the population of Arabia remained very small through the centuries. From time to time, one tribe or another would win control over neighboring tribes and form "a kingdom," but it in turn would soon be overthrown.

ISLAM: CENTER OF SAUDI LIFE

In the sixth century, Arabia moved from the fringe of world civilizations to the center of a major religion. The new religious movement began in the town of Mecca, an important trading center on the caravan route from the Gulf of Aden to Egypt and Damascus. There, in Mecca, the greatest and last prophet of Islam was born.

Mecca was already an important center of worship for pagan Arabs. As Muslims still do today, the Arabs worshipped a sacred black stone, the Ka'ba, said to have been given to Adam, the first man in the Bible, when he was forced from the Garden of Eden.

The people of Mecca worshipped many gods, but there were Jewish and Christian traders in the town as well. Muhammad, the prophet of Islam, rejected the pagan religion of his tribe and, as a merchant, studied the Christianity and Judaism of the merchants who came to Mecca.

In A.D. 620, when he was about 40 years old, Muhammad had the first of many visions—the angel Gabriel is believed to have come to him and told him "to recite for the Lord." Muhammad, who was illiterate, became a prophet for the god he called Allah, who was the god of Jews and Christians, as well. Muhammad also saw Abraham, Moses, other Old Testament figures, and Jesus Christ as prophets. Muslims recognize Muhammad as the last and greatest prophet of God. He had a new message—the last word of God. Muhammad told the people of his tribe in Mecca to give up their pagan gods and accept the will of Allah. They not only refused, but forced Muhammad to leave the city. He fled to Medina, another trading town some 280 miles (450 kilometers) to the northeast, in 622. (The Muslim calendar begins with that year.) There, his message was well received.

THE MUSLIM CALENDAR

The Muslim calendar is very different from that of the West. For Muslims, dates begin with Muhammad's departure from Mecca (July 15, 622). The Muslim year is lunar; it is based on the cycles of the moon. Since each cycle consists of 29½ days, the 12-month Muslim year is 354 days long (not 365). Every 30 years, the Muslim calendar has an extra day, like a leap year.

Because the Muslim year is 11 days shorter than a year based on Earth's rotation around the sun, the months gradually shift through the seasons. Over 33 years, a Muslim month will shift through the entire yearly seasonal cycle. For example, the month of Ramadan, when Muslims fast during daylight hours, will occur in all the seasons over 33 years. Since the observance of Ramadan requires complete fasting, including no liquid, during daylight hours, the duration of the fasting is greater in the summer than in the winter.

The days of the Muslim calendar are not determined by tables of the movement of the moon, but by the actual sighting of the moon, or daylight and sunset. Night begins when it becomes so dark that one cannot tell a white thread from a black one. Like any other month, Ramadan begins when the first new moon is sighted. In Riyadh during Ramadan, a cannon is fired to announce daybreak and sundown each day.

MUHAMMAD, MEDINA, AND EMPIRE

Muhammad preached that God was ruler of the earth. Humans do not make laws; they must obey the laws of God as revealed to Muhammad. The people of Medina soon accepted the Prophet Muhammad's teachings and, as God's messenger, he ruled the town. He urged his followers to spread Allah's word to the world. Eight years later, he and his fervent Muslim believers had conquered Mecca. When Muhammad died in 632, he and his followers had spread his message across the deserts of Arabia. They had converted the desert tribes and established one government over most of the Arabian Peninsula. Within 12 years of his death, Muhammad's followers—most of them Arab nomads and townspeople—controlled most of the Middle East. Only what is now Turkey was not a part of the Muslim empire.

This rapid conquest was carried out by Arabs from the Arabian Peninsula who were driven by the power of their new religion and their enthusiasm for it. They were fighting a holy war to spread the word of God. They also were Bedouins, used to living under difficult conditions. They knew how to fight, because they had regularly raided towns with populations larger than their own. They also knew the desert and, using camels and horses, moved forward along its edges to strike towns and villages. Their reputation as fierce fighters often encouraged communities to give up without a fight.

The Arabs conquered the Middle East, but they did not intend to destroy it. They wanted two things: to spread Islam and to collect taxes from the occupied lands.

THE SPREAD OF EMPIRE

During the next 500 years, Islamic forces spread across North Africa all the way to the Atlantic Ocean, and by the early eighth century, had moved into southern Spain. They were defeated in southern France while trying to move farther into western

Europe. In the Middle East, they pushed back the Christian Byzantine Empire in Turkey and conquered the Persian Empire. The fierce Mogul tribesmen of central Asia (today, the 'stan countries that were formerly Muslim-dominated Soviet Socialist Republics) converted to Islam and spread their empire across Afghanistan into northwest India. Arabic traders sailed eastward across the Indian Ocean to bring Islam to the East Indies (now Indonesia, Malaysia, and the Philippines). By now, these forces, though still Muslim, were no longer led by Arabs, but by peoples they had converted to Islam.

The great Islamic empire of the past is gone. Even as it grew, power shifted from Arabia to Baghdad, Cairo, and other centers outside of Arabia. Still, the impact of what happened in Mecca and Medina dominates the Islamic world today.

THE TEACHINGS OF MUHAMMAD

Muhammad could not write, but his version of the words of God was collected in what became the holy book of Islam, the Koran. For Muslims, the Koran is the holy word of God, just as the Torah and the Bible are for Jews and Christians. The Koran, as interpreted by Islamic leaders, sets the rules of life for its believers, and for business and government in places that are Muslim. The Koran and the collected sayings of Muhammad (the hadith) form the basis of Muslim law in countries where Islam is the official religion.

Muslim law applies to every part of daily life for individuals: what they eat and drink, how they behave at home and at work, and how they interact with one another. The Koran tells a Muslim what he or she can or cannot do. Muslims follow it because it is considered God's law, not law created by humans. The main concern of government in Saudi Arabia is to enforce God's law. The House of Saud considers the Koran its constitution. Of course, it is humans who interpret God's word in the Koran, thereby making God's law subject to many different interpretations throughout the Muslim world.

Not only was Islam founded by an Arab, but the Koran was written in the Arabic language. As a result, Arabic has become the written language used in many of the countries that make up the Islamic world today, even though Muslims in different areas may speak other languages. Muhammad's teachings are not restricted only to the Koran. Another important Islamic system called the *Sunnah*, or "the way," is consulted alongside the teachings of the Koran. Sunnah refers to the life and times of Muhammad; thus, Islam asks people to model their life based on his own personal activities, because this would enable a Muslim to live a righteous way.

Both the Koran and Sunnah are indispensable in all aspects of Saudi society, particularly in governance and the legal system. In many cases, another scripture called the hadith is also studied together with the Koran. Hadith is a narration of Muhammad's action, whereas Sunnah is the complete work on his life. The practice of Islam in the Saudi culture is linked very closely with the practice of Sunnah and consulting the Koran for prayer and worship. Accordingly, some parts of Sunnah are *wajib* (obligatory), while some are *mustahaab* (encouraged). Muslims are required to follow the Sunnah, whether it is wajib or mustahaab, and its practice is closely monitored by the Islamic scholars, or *ulemas*, in every Saudi Arabian settlement region.

THE HOLY CITIES AND THE HAJJ

Wherever they are in the world, devout Muslims pray five times a day, facing in the direction of Mecca. All Muslims are supposed to make one pilgrimage to Mecca, where a great mosque surrounds the ancient black rock—the *Ka'ba*. Each year, some 3 to 4 million Muslims visit Mecca. The most sacred pilgrimage occurs between the seventh and tenth days of the holy month of Dhu'l Hijja, the time when Muhammad fled from Mecca to Medina. Each pilgrim wears the same white seamless gown, a symbol that all Muslims, rich or poor, are equal in the sight of Allah.

Each year, between 3 and 4 million Muslims make the pilgrimage to Mecca, where they perform a series of ritual acts. Here, Muslim pilgrims perform Friday prayers near the Namira Mosque at Mount Arafat, southeast of the Saudi holy city of Mecca, on the first day of the hajj in 2006.

The pilgrimage in Mecca lasts for a week. It is made up of both solemn worship and celebration and feasting. Handling so many pilgrims over such a short period of time is a tremendous challenge for Saudi Arabia. All the pilgrims must be transported, fed, and housed. Most enter the country through the port city of Jiddah on the Red Sea. They come by boat and plane, and then must be transported some 50 miles to Mecca. Most pilgrims live in tent villages during their stay in the holy city. It is an enormous task to feed them all, provide sanitation and places to sleep, and even to communicate with people coming from foreign countries. Medical and first-aid facilities must also be provided, and the pilgrims must be guided through the many steps of the *hajj*, as the pilgrimage is called.

The House of Saud is very proud to be the homeland of the Prophet Muhammad. Its members see their responsibility for assisting the pilgrims on the hajj as a God-given duty. At the same time, visiting pilgrims provide an important source of income for the people of the Jiddah-Mecca-Medina area.

STATUS OF WOMEN

One of the striking observations a first-time visitor to Saudi Arabia would notice is the status of its women. The country has restricted women's rights to the degree that it has raised concerns among international human rights organizations for many years. Saudi Arabia is the most conservative Muslim nation in terms of providing equal opportunity to women. But in recent years, there have been several movements leading to protests by women seeking equality. The plight of Saudi women was brought to international attention when, in the 2005 elections, the Saudi Interior Ministry prevented women from running for office or even participating in the voting process.

Besides voting rights, there are strict rules in place that monitor women's movements. For instance, Sharia law requires that women in public be accompanied by a male escort at all times. According to the law, the escort can be any male member related either by marriage or birth. It is critical for women to move about with a male companion. In the event a woman is seen without an escort, she can be arrested (or worse). The *Mutawa'een*, or religious police force, is given the task of ensuring that women behave in accordance with Sharia laws. The Mutawa'een reports only to the king and thus has an almost immeasurable amount of power. Women's restrictions extend even to driving. They are not allowed to drive cars, and in recent times they have not even been allowed to drive golf carts.

Despite the many restrictions, the Koran, through Sharia law, grants equal economic rights to women. Women are legally entitled to inherit and give away property. They are also allowed to hold wealth and property in their own names after marriage. In recent years, the government has promoted better educational facilities for girls and young women. In urban regions, including Riyadh and Jiddah, young women can even be seen dressed in Western attire. Change is coming, but, as is true with most aspects of society and culture, only very gradually within Saudi Arabia.

SAUDI DINING AND DIET

An important element of any culture is its cuisine. Located strategically between Asia Minor and South Asia, Saudi Arabia has been at the crossroads of food diffusion for thousands of years. The western province of Hejaz is probably the best region that illustrates the diversity that food has brought into Saudi society. Here, the ideal location of Mecca, Medina, and Jiddah, and the access to Egypt and northern Arab nations has promoted a unique mixture of ingredients and food styles, many of which have blended together. In early times, especially during the expansion of Islam, caravans loaded with spices, bread, and meat traveled across the dry, barren deserts. Muslim pilgrims traveling to Mecca met people from their faith from throughout the Islamic world, further allowing the region to become a melting pot of cultures and their food. Bedouins in this region adapted to the ways of the desert with their innovative bread-making techniques. Since Muslims are prohibited from eating pork, camel and goat meat are very popular. In the Hejaz, the unique cuisine is quite popular. A typical meal includes the *harisah*, a meat dish with sugared wheat, along with *jubniyyah*, a dessert made of goat's milk, and *lahuh*, crepes with meat and sour cream or yogurt. For a first-time visitor to Saudi Arabia, it would not be surprising if Saudi people were to greet him or her and provide a lavish meal. Almost every meal is accompanied by *kubez* bread, which is flat and unleavened. Saudi foodways vary in other parts of the nation, with people adapting to the harsh ways of the arid climate. For example, in the southern parts of the nation, use of stone is common to promote slow cooking. This helps caravan riders and desert travelers to cook while moving along the treacherous desert valleys. On the eastern coast of the nation, seafood is quite common. In recent times, with many South Asians working in construction companies in the eastern provinces, rice has become popular as well. *Al-Sayadiah*, which is made of fish cooked with rice and onions, is one of the most popular Saudi dishes of this region.

Arabic Coffee: A Saudi Tradition

Saudi cuisine is incomplete without coffee. Because alcohol is prohibited by the Koran, Arabic coffee is not only popular among its people, but it has become one of the most popular beverages throughout the world. Saudi Arabia's proximity to Ethiopia, the birthplace of coffee, has helped preserve some traditional blends for several thousands of years. For a Saudi, coffee is not only a beverage. Coffee making, or *gawha*, is a fine art and an important custom. In gawha, the host prepares coffee for the guest fresh from the beans, roasted and ground in front of them. A traditional Bedouin way of making coffee is to add cardamom while grinding the coffee beans, then serving the freshly brewed coffee with unsweetened dates.

5

Government and Politics

A rab leadership of the Islamic empire did not last long. There were too few desert people to maintain control. The new leadership came from the ancient agricultural civilizations in Egypt, Mesopotamia, and Persia (present-day Iran). There, Muslim converts became the rulers of great new Muslim civilizations.

RETURN TO THE BEDOUIN LIFE

With their empire in disarray, many Arabs returned to their nomadic desert lifestyle, but continued to maintain their strong belief in Islam. There was no single government on the Arabian Peninsula. The people remained separated into different tribes, each with its own sheik and its own part of the desert, which they defended with great ferocity. For hundreds of years, the tribes of the Arabian Peninsula were almost completely isolated from the rest of the world.

They were few, very poor by world standards, and deeply suspicious of outsiders.

The holy cities of Mecca and Medina had a different history, because they were so important to all the world's Muslims. They were first part of Egypt, and then part of the Turkish Ottoman Empire. The holy cities were on the outer fringe of these empires, however, so the local Arab leader, the *sharif* of Mecca, was largely in control. Eventually, he became powerful among the very religious Arabian tribes.

THE ROOTS OF SAUDI ARABIA

By about 1750, a religious leader in central Arabia, named Muhammad ibn Abd al-Wahhab, began to teach a very strict type of Islam. After traveling through the Middle East, he felt that Muslims had strayed from the true teachings of the Prophet Muhammad. The form of Islam he preached was called *Wahhabism*, after its founder. Wahhabism spread through the tribes of Arabia, and Wahhab's followers began a struggle against the form of Islam practiced in the Turkish-controlled Ottoman Empire. Wabbahism further isolated Arabia from the centers of power in the Middle East. Early in the nineteenth century, the Wahhabis captured Mecca and ruled it for several years, until the Turks again took over all of northwestern Arabia, including both Mecca and Medina.

Wahhabism and its very strict interpretation of Islam remains the form most Saudis practice today. In Islamic Saudi Arabia, there is no separation of church and state. The king is seen as God's representative on Earth and the caretaker of the holy cities. The king consults a council of religious leaders on all major governmental decisions. Although Wahhabi values fit the way of life of Arabia's Bedouins, Wahhabism has presented difficulties for the present Saudi government as it works to bring the country into the modern world. For the Wahhabis, the world should ideally be kept as much like the world of the Prophet Muhammad's time as possible.

Ibn Saud, who is known as Abdul Aziz in Saudi Arabia, became ruler of Saudi Arabia in 1932 after defeating several opposing factions. Ibn Saud is pictured here in the 1930s with his son Saud bin Abdul Aziz, who became king after his father's death in 1953.

THE HOUSE OF SAUD

The history of Saudi Arabia is not only that of Wahhabi Islam, but also that of the Saud family. The family comes from a town in the Nadj, 10 miles north of the present capital of

Riyadh. Its members were supporters of the Wahhabi movement and gained power over other tribes with the help of its religious message.

Near the end of the nineteenth century, the Sauds were forced to flee the country and take refuge in Kuwait. According to legend, Ibn Saud (known in Arabia as Abdul Aziz), who would later establish the Saudi Kingdom, was smuggled away in a basket slung from a camel as the family fled.

In 1901, as an adult, Ibn Saud led a small band of men who captured the small town of Riyadh from another tribe. By 1912, he controlled the entire interior of Arabia. His goal was to capture Mecca and Medina. In 1924, he walked into Mecca. Wearing a seamless white robe, he entered the city not as a conqueror, but as a pilgrim. By 1932, he had taken control of most of the Arabian Peninsula and named his new kingdom Saudi Arabia, using his family name.

King Ibn Saud died in 1953. Since then, all of the rulers of Saudi Arabia have come from the House of Saud. The king does not rule alone; rather, he consults with the other members of his family, who form the inner circle of Saudi society. All the kings of Saudi Arabia to this day have been sons of Ibn Saud. Princes hold the key positions in the Saudi government under the king. Ibn Saud alone produced a vast number of offspring—45 sons by 22 wives. This was part of his strategy to unite the tribes into one country. Each of his many wives came from a different tribe. (Islam allows multiple wives if the husband is able to provide them with adequate financial and other support.) Today, there are more than 5,000 members of the Saudi royal family.

THE FAMILY RULES

Because there is no parliament or other democratic body, the king is considered an absolute ruler. What he says is law. In practice, however, things do not always work out this way. The king's decisions must be acceptable to the House of Saud, particularly his many brothers, many of whom hold prominent positions in the government.

The authority of the king—and his brother princes—rests on a legacy of being children or grandchildren of the country's founder, Ibn Saud. Those who are closest to the "roots" of the family tree have the choicest positions and the most influence. The individuals who are further removed from the main family have less important government positions, or may be in charge of some major business or military force.

Foreigners doing business in Saudi Arabia know that it is important to have a connection to a member of the House of Saud. The wealthy Arab merchants and businessmen know this, too. Most of the rich made their fortunes through their connections to the House of Saud. Business is done in Saudi Arabia through personal connections, and there are no better connections to have than those with the Saud family.

Although Saudi Arabia has no representative government, the Saud family does not have absolute control. Its members depend on a wide consensus, both within the family and with the leading religious leaders (the ulema) of the Wahhabi sect, many of whom have married into the Saud family. The Council of Ministers who advise the king include a few key princes and religious leaders, as well as a number of senior government bureaucrats. In 2000, the king established a family council of 18 senior princes to select future kings and to foster better relations between members of the royal family.

Because all important Saudi decisions are made by the House of Saud and the Wahhabi ulema, there is growing discontent among the educated Saudi commoners who work in the government and business. In recent years, the House of Saud has allowed these so-called technocrats to fill important government posts. However, princes of the House of Saud still control the key positions—defense, foreign affairs, and interior—in the king's cabinet.

STILL TRIBAL RULE

Ibn Saud began as a local sheik who ruled by consent of the members of his tribe. In an Arab tribe, every member can directly approach the sheik about any concern, or to ask a favor. One of Ibn Saud's favorite quotations was, "The chief of a tribe is its servant." When he became king, he actually became the sheik over the sheiks of all the local tribes.

Ibn Saud lived a simple life and spent much of his time traveling from tribe to tribe with government records and the treasury in boxes, or receiving the sheiks in his palace in Riyadh. Any Saudi could visit the king to file a complaint; get a meal; obtain a dagger, cloak, or sack of sugar; dictate a marriage contract; have ailments treated; or hear Wahhabi scholars recite from the Koran. Almost every day, the king held *majlis* (a reception) for anyone who wished to speak with him. Often he would feed several hundred such people.

To an extent, the Saudi government still works in this way. It has become a welfare state, based on favors from the House of Saud. Saudi people get free education through the college level, and even graduate school, either within the country or abroad. Health care, including dental and eye care and prescriptions, is essentially free. Money is provided for those who need special treatment outside the country. Basic foods, such as grains, sugar, and milk, are subsidized, as are housing and utilities. Farmers and businesses receive grants and interest-free loans. Land on which to build homes has been given away. Land, cars, and trucks were given to Bedouins to encourage them to abandon their nomadic life and move into cities. A social security system is provided for the elderly and the disabled.

SAUDIS IN MODERN SOCIETY

The result of all this has left Saudis with little incentive to work. Some, of course, will rush into a business in which they may become wealthy. However, few Saudis like to work for others, or to work regular hours. They do not want to do the kind of physical work needed in the many construction projects—in the oil fields, on the road or airports, or building housing projects and other structures in the country's booming cities—that are converting Saudi Arabia into a modern nation. They leave that type of work for foreign laborers, who are not, and never can be, Saudis, and who cannot reap the benefits of the welfare state. Foreigners, even if they are Muslims, are expected to do their jobs, be paid, live in compounds away from regular Saudi life, and then leave the country when their jobs are done.

CHANGING POLITICAL SCENE

Saudi Arabian society is diverse and Islamic ideologies vary throughout the nation. A monotheistic religion such as Islam finds two opposing traditions. For example, there are two major groups of Saudis who differ vastly in their adherence to Islamic faith and its practice. On one hand, there is the *Tawhid* school of Islam, which promotes conservative monotheistic Islam as defined by Muhammad ibn al-Wahhab, who is also credited as the founder of Wahhabism. Tawhid Muslims in Western religious definitions would be considered a conservative traditional sect. The group supports absolute Wahabbi Islam and maintains close relationship with the *jihad,* or struggle in establishing the foundations of Islamic faith. Muslim clerics enjoy great autonomy and power thanks to Tawhid, which promotes the strict guidelines defined by the Koran. In fact, Tawhid grants political status to Muslim clerics, who often assume a leadership role in governing, especially in the rural interior.

Prince Nayef, the half brother of King Abdullah, is a key adherent of Tawhid Islam and controls the Commission for the Promotion of Virtue and Prevention of Vice. The commission recently garnered the world's attention when schoolgirls who apparently did not wear proper Islamic attire were beaten with batons. Prince Nayef has denied these allegations.

On the other extreme side of the Islamic values spectrum is *Taqarub* Islam, espoused by King Abdullah, who is seen as

In August 2005, Abdullah bin Abdul Aziz Al Saud became king of Saudi Arabia, succeeding his half brother Fahd. Since he became ruler, King Abdullah (right), who is pictured here with Crown Prince Sultan bin Abdul Aziz shortly after giving a speech condemning a recent al-Qaeda attack in April 2007, has attempted to crack down on terrorist groups in Saudi Arabia.

its key follower. Political plurality and coexistence with non-Muslims are some of the ideologies of Taqarub Islam, which is much different than the ultratraditional Tawhid school of Islam. King Abdullah's Taqarub approach has attracted international admiration for his promotion of feminism, secularism, and coexistence of Jewish Israelis, as well as Shia Muslims.

King Abdullah as Liberal Reformer

With respect to his role in maintaining close ties between the Western and Islamic worlds, King Abdullah favors open dialogue with these potential allies and trade partners. For instance, King Abdullah's open dialog approach has led to his formulation of a peace plan to end the ongoing Israeli-Palestinian conflict. In his "Saudi Peace Plan," the king suggested the complete withdrawal of Israeli forces from Gaza, the West Bank, and East Jerusalem. The Israeli government has recently favored this plan, as has much of the international community. The Tawhid followers on the other hand may not support this process, but Saudi Arabia's influence over the Israel-Palestine situation will continue in one way or the other.

POLITICS AND RELIGION: STRIKING THE BALANCE

Saudi governance under King Abdullah has also tried to strike a balance between the political administration and the religious establishments. Recent reforms in the Saudi Arabian government represent a positive trend in the political processes of the kingdom nation. For example, for the first time since the 1960s, Saudi municipal elections were held in 2005. This was seen as an initial step toward the promotion of democracy by King Abdullah's regime. However, women were barred from voting, a decision that raised concern among human rights organizations. The king, however, promised that by 2009 women would be allowed to vote.

Another important component of Saudi governance is the Shura Council. The 150-member council oversees the implementation of Sharia law, with the government's support. The Shura Council is a key advisory body to the king and is made up of several committees chaired by members nominated by the king and the House of Saud.

6

Saudi Arabia's Economy

I t was the discovery of oil in the 1930s, just after the country was created, that thrust Saudi Arabia into the modern world. Actually, the first important oil discovery in the Middle East was by the crew of an Australian investor in Persia (now Iran) 25 years earlier—in 1908. This was the first well in the world's greatest oil-producing basin, which extends in and around the Persian Gulf. That basin is shared by the countries around the gulf: Iran, Iraq, Kuwait, Bahrain, the United Arab Emirates, Oman, and Saudi Arabia. The basin includes more than half of the world's known oil reserves still in the ground. Saudi Arabia, alone, has more than half of these vast Persian Gulf reserves.

In Persia, pipelines were built to bring the oil to the gulf, and a refinery was built along the coast. Oil from the Persian fields supplied fuel for the British Navy during World War I. In 1927, oil was found in Iraq by European oil companies. In 1932, oil was discovered on the island of Bahrain, and geologists wanted to explore the lands of Kuwait and Saudi Arabia.

PERMISSION TO DRILL

Companies could not simply go exploring wherever they hoped to find oil. The countries of the Persian Gulf were sovereign states. The oil companies made deals that allowed them to drill in particular areas. As part of these so-called concessions granted by the government, the oil company paid royalties (a share of the price of each barrel produced) to the government.

King Abdul Aziz had offered a concession in Arabia in 1923, even before the nation had been created, but wells were never drilled. By the 1930s, U.S. oil companies were very interested in exploring the new country of Saudi Arabia. However, it was a time of great worldwide economic difficulty, called the Great Depression. Banks were having problems, and loans were hard to obtain. Oil was selling for 50¢ a barrel (during the summer of 2006, it was selling for more than $78 a barrel). An agreement was signed in 1933 that provided the Saudis with about a dollar for every ton of oil produced, plus yearly land rent of about $25,000. Provisions called for immediate exploration and the construction of a refinery once oil was discovered.

EXPLORING

The first area explored was what geologists called the Dammam Dome, named for a nearby village. Today, Ad Dammam is a city of about 750,000 people and the oil capital of Saudi Arabia.

To aid geological mapping, a single-engine high-winged airplane was equipped with extra gas tanks and a big camera. Because of strict Wahhabi concerns about modern conveniences, the government insisted that the plane fly high and use no radio. Blowing sand often grounded it, and it needed large tires to land on the sandy surface.

In 1938, oil was discovered in Saudi Arabia at Dammam Dome No. 7, and today there are 52 oil fields throughout the country. Pictured here in 1945 is one of the country's first wells, al-Qatif, which is located in northeastern Saudi Arabia.

Before the first well could be drilled, bunkhouses had to be built and a pier erected to unload supplies. The first well did not produce enough oil to be used, but it did provide gas for cooking and enough power to drill other wells. After 15 months of drilling, the seventh well was a commercial success. The Saudi government received an advance of $50,000. In 1939, the first oil tanker was loaded at a new harbor on the Persian Gulf, with the Saudi king looking on.

Throughout the 1930s, geologic exploration increased the size of the known oil field. Geologists found the world's largest oil accumulation in a field more than 160 miles (258 kilometers) long and 20 miles (32 kilometers) wide. To provide the funding and technical know-how needed to handle all of this oil, the Arabian American Oil Company (ARAMCO) was formed. In addition to Standard Oil of California (SOCO) and Texaco, the original drilling companies, the Standard Oil companies of New York (Esso, now Exxon) and New Jersey (Socony-Vacuum, then Mobil) were added. World War II broke out in 1939 and when the United States became involved in 1941, all operations ceased.

OIL PRODUCTION SOARS

After World War II, production began to soar again. The demand for oil was growing rapidly, and Saudi Arabia was emerging as the most important exporter. Not only were geologists uncovering the world's largest oil deposits there, but the production costs were also very low.

In Saudi Arabia, the House of Saud owned almost all of the land, and ARAMCO was the only company pumping. A few wells could be strategically located in each field. Large wells could be spaced miles apart. Each well fed into the same network of collecting pipelines, all of which led to one storage facility. Other important wells in Saudi Arabia flow freely to the surface without the need for pumping.

Even though Saudi Arabia was far from the major world oil markets in North America, Europe, and Japan, shipment by ocean tankers was not expensive. A whole new deepwater seaport, Ras Tanura, was constructed on the Persian Gulf, and a short pipeline brought oil to a second shipping port on the island country of Bahrain. The member companies of ARAMCO wanted to pump all the oil they could.

SAUDI OIL

Today, oil and natural gas are produced from some 77 different fields in Saudi Arabia and in the neutral zone the country shares with Kuwait. The ARAMCO oil-drilling concession covers some 85,000 square miles (220,150 square kilometers), extending about 250 miles (400 kilometers) north, west, and south of the headquarters at the new city of Ad Dammam. It has reserves of more than 75 billion barrels, more than three times the total of all known oil fields in the United States. Oil is also pumped from the largest offshore oil field in the Persian Gulf. It has almost as much oil as the total reserves of the United States.

Saudi oil varies from one field to another. Some is light, some heavy, some "sour" (full of sulfur), and some "sweet" (sulfur-free). Light oils produce more gasoline and high-grade products; heavy oil produces more tar and asphalt. Oil in the ground is also associated with natural gas. For many years, gas could be piped to cities and factories in Saudi Arabia, but it was very difficult to ship by tanker. Most of the gas in Saudi fields was "flared"—burned off in the air. Today, sophisticated gas tankers have been built, but its volatility makes natural gas much more dangerous to ship than oil.

BUILDING THE OIL-PRODUCING SYSTEM

Although oil was plentiful and easy to reach, in the early decades of production, Saudi Arabia remained a very primitive country, and the desert environment was a very difficult place to work. An entire infrastructure had to be built, not just wells, pipelines, storage facilities, and shipping ports. Roads and housing for thousands of workers had to be constructed. All materials for starting the wells, oil-collecting pipelines, storage tanks, and ports had to be brought in from North America and Europe. All the food and other needs of workers had to be imported.

Warehouses, shops, recreation facilities, and offices also were built. And all construction had to be done in the hostile desert environment. All of this added an expensive dimension to oil operations. By 1970, there were about 10,000 workers; by 1980, the number was four times that. Today, there are an estimated 7.2 million foreign workers in Saudi Arabia. Not all of them, of course, work in the oil industry, but an estimated 50 percent of all oil field laborers are non-Saudis.

SHIPPING OIL IN THE PERSIAN GULF

Oil production in eastern Saudi Arabia was on the wrong side of the peninsula to easily serve the North American and European markets. Moreover, Iran—certainly no friend to either Saudi Arabia or the United States—lay along one side of the narrow Strait of Hormuz that separates the Persian Gulf and the Gulf of Oman. During the 1980s, Iran threatened to close the strait and attacked oil tankers in the Persian Gulf.

To overcome the problems of shipment from the Persian Gulf, two pipelines were built across the Arabian Peninsula. The Trans-Arabian Pipeline (TAP) in the north ran just outside the Iraqi border, across Jordan, to the ancient port of Sidon in Lebanon. When wars between Arab countries and Israel threatened the TAP, a second pipeline was built across the middle of Saudi Arabia to the new port of Yanbu. These were the largest privately financed construction projects in the world at the time. Two additional pipelines—one for oil and one for gas—were later laid parallel to the one from the oil fields to Yanbu. Even with these pipelines, most Saudi oil is shipped from Persian Gulf ports. A second shipping port was created at Ju'aymah, 15 miles (24 kilometers) north of Ras Tanura. Some 4,500 tankers are loaded each year.

Today, Saudi Arabia has four pipelines that transport oil from the interior to port cites such as Yanbu and Ju'aymah. Pictured here is a worker standing next to a pipeline at the ARAMCO oil field complex at Shaybah, in the Ar Rub al-Khali.

CONTROL OF OIL PRODUCTION

The ruling House of Saud holds the rights to all the minerals in the country. In the early days of oil exploration, the country had no way of producing oil itself, so it offered the concession to explore to ARAMCO. In return, the House of Saud received royalties. As the global market for oil expanded after 1950, the royalty increased to 50 percent of the sale price of each gallon sold. Then, in 1988, the House of Saud took complete control of ARAMCO from the American companies. The Saud-controlled government now also owns the refineries and shipping facilities. ARAMCO also operates a fleet of more than 30 oil tankers and owns storage facilities in the Netherlands, Singapore, and in the Caribbean Sea.

The growth of Saudi oil production has been phenomenal. From 500,000 barrels a day at the end of 1949, it rose to 4.8 million a day in 1971, to almost 10 million barrels a day in 1980. Since then, production has shifted markedly up and down, varying with demand.

As the world's leading oil exporter, Saudi Arabia has attempted to stabilize world oil prices, or to use oil prices as a political tool. In 1960, it joined with other major oil countries to form the Organization of Petroleum Exporting Countries (OPEC), in which Saudi Arabia and its oil-producing neighbors around the Persian Gulf—Iran, Iraq, Kuwait, Qatar, and the United Arab Emirates—are joined by Arab oil producers in North Africa—Libya and Algeria—as well as Nigeria, Venezuela, and Indonesia. The group meets regularly to set quotas for each member country that will help world oil prices stay within a range that will suit OPEC nations. Saudi Arabia's oil production, more than twice that of any other OPEC member, more or less determines OPEC's output. The problem for OPEC is that other major world oil exporters –Mexico, Norway, Russia, Canada, and Malaysia—are not members. This means that OPEC cannot completely control prices.

AN ECONOMY DEPENDENT ON OIL

Since its discovery more than 70 years ago, oil has produced more than U.S. $1 trillion for the Saudi treasury. This is an impressive figure for a country that, in 1950, was thought to have only about 6 million people and only slightly more than double that number today. At that time, Jiddah, the port nearest to the holy cities of Mecca and Medina, was the only real city in the country. About half the people were nomadic Bedouins, living in tents and herding camels and goats. Most of the rest were oasis farmers trying to support themselves on date palms and small plots of grain. The chief exports were dates and Arabian horses. Arabia's chief contact with the outside world was with the hajj tourists to Mecca. Taxes paid by the pilgrims were an important source of income for the House of Saud.

In this remote part of the world, slavery was not abolished until 1962. The first paved road—between Jiddah and Riyadh, the capital—was completed in 1967. Riyadh, an old walled city with about 30,000 people, remained intact until after World War II. The city consisted of two- and three-story adobe buildings with flat roofs. The tallest structure was a water tower. The streets were dry and dusty. There were open-air markets with tin-roofed and dirt-floored stalls; vendors cooked chickens over fires along the sidewalks. Nomads brought their flocks to the city with them. Public beheadings were held in the square.

The first Saudi king, Ibn Saud, kept the treasury in a trunk that he carried with him when he visited different Bedouin tribes. He handed out sums to individuals who brought their pleas to him. He regularly brought the local sheiks to Riyadh to receive religious instruction, and to keep their loyalty, he gave them subsidies. The government levied almost no taxes. Money came from taxes on pilgrims and from the British, who wanted to ensure that the Suez Canal–Red Sea route to India be kept open. When the first oil money began to flow into the treasury, the government did little with it. Other than building a few wells and a pier for the ships bringing pilgrims to Mecca, it spent nothing on roads, electricity, telephones, or any other part of a modern infrastructure.

WHAT TO DO WITH IT ALL

The oil money began to arrive in vast amounts after the mid-1950s. In 1970, annual oil sales equaled more than $500 for each person in the nation; by 1980, the amount was more than

$11,000. Today, the figure is much higher. Of course, the money all went into the treasury of the House of Saud.

Some of it was used to support a lavish lifestyle for all the extended Saud family. Some was invested in banks, businesses, and real estate in the United States and Europe. Then, the House of Saud decided to move its country into the twentieth century. The first five-year plan, in 1970, was designed by Western economists who had been hired by the Saud family. More than $8 billion was to be spent, most of it on modernizing the largest Saudi cities, Jiddah and Medina, with streets, modern utilities, schools and hospitals, housing, and airports. Money was also to be spent on a modern defense organization complete with jet fighters and tanks. Other five-year plans followed, and expanded the settled areas of the country.

THE WORLD'S LARGEST CONSTRUCTION SITE

During this period, Saudi Arabia became a gigantic construction site. Because the country had no factories to produce the construction materials, no engineers to make the plans, and no workers trained to handle modern equipment, the entire massive national development project had to be put into the hands of businesses and workers from outside the country. Contracts for the projects were given to large global construction companies from the United States, Europe, and Japan. The companies established project headquarters staffed by their engineers. Workers were recruited from other Arab countries—Egypt, Yemen, Sudan, Lebanon, and Pakistan—and from the Pacific Rim countries of Korea, the Philippines, and Thailand. They were hired by the tens of thousands. Airports had to be expanded to handle their arrival, and housing for them had to be created on the construction sites. So much equipment was coming in through the few ports that ships had to wait offshore for weeks, or even months, before they could be unloaded. In the midst of this, the government also had to manage its new social programs. A wide array of departments—agriculture, defense, communications, finance, health, industry and electricity, interior, justice, petroleum and mineral resources, planning, public works, and housing—had to be organized by outsiders until the Saudis could get the education needed to handle the duties.

CONTROLLING FOREIGN WORKERS

The masses of foreigners, many of them non-Muslims, presented problems for the Saudi government. Islam has rules for everyday life—what to wear, what to eat, what to drink, and how to behave. Islam prohibited eating pork or drinking alcohol. The ways of the non-Muslims, particularly the Westerners who were in charge of the new construction projects and government agencies, were very different. The government decided to segregate the Westerners as much as possible. They were placed in housing compounds, with their own schools and recreation. When they left the compounds, they were expected to follow Islamic customs.

OIL'S IMPACT ON SAUDI SOCIETY

All this brought changes in the life of Saudi people, the majority of whom were Bedouins or conservative Muslims. Bedouins moved to the city, sometimes pitching their tents in any open space and grazing their flocks in the new public parks. In the cities, Western goods began to appear in shops; cars and trucks crowded the streets; fast-food stores, supermarkets, and fashionable boutiques replaced the open markets and street vendors. Modern schools replaced religious schools where the curriculum had centered on the Koran. Saudi young people were sent to universities in Europe and the United States to learn engineering, economics and business, and international relations (including geography), to help their country move into the modern world.

As part of the new development plans, all Saudis were given free education, health care, and social security. The government subsidized basic food needs, absorbing much of the cost of expensive food imports. Bedouins were offered free land, cheap

In Saudi Arabian cities such as Mecca, the wealth generated from oil has led to an influx of Western goods and services. Here, Muslim pilgrims gather in a Kentucky Fried Chicken near Mecca's Grand Mosque, shortly before the hajj.

irrigation water, and interest-free loans to buy machinery, seed, and fertilizer if they would settle on new farms. Others were given trucks or taxicabs.

The benefits of the new Saudi Arabia were restricted to its people only. None of the programs were available to foreign workers. Foreign workers are considered temporary residents. They are expected to leave the country when their contract ends. The Saudis expected that, over time, the construction would slow, and Saudis would take over the work. Then, Saudi Arabia would be made up almost exclusively of Arabs.

However, the foreigners have not gone home. Even now, foreigners make up one-third of the population and a larger share of the workforce. There have been problems educating enough Saudis to take over all the management positions. It has been even harder to get Saudis to do everyday tasks: repairing the machines and doing maintenance work and heavy labor.

Faced with the continuing importance of foreigners to the Saudi economy, in recent years the House of Saud has tried to bring change. First, it has increased the training of Saudis so that they can take over many of the jobs now being done by foreigners. Second, it has begun to make some concessions to foreign workers. Foreigners may now own land, and a compulsory health-care plan has been started for them.

USING OIL MONEY TO BROADEN THE ECONOMY

As development plans moved forward, the House of Saud pushed to use its rich oil resources as a base for creating industry. The idea was to use the vast supply of cheap energy, particularly natural gas, which was being wasted as it flared in the oil fields. The first step was to build oil refineries, not only to supply the Saudi economy, but to ship higher-value products such as gasoline and jet fuel instead of the lower-value crude oil. Refineries also produce a wide variety of by-products that can be made into oil-based chemicals, called petrochemicals. Why not build refineries and petrochemical plants and pipe the derivatives of the refinery directly to the petrochemical plants? Today, Saudi Arabia has eight refineries and several petrochemical plants. Most are located along the Gulf coast near the oil fields.

The problem is that, although Saudi Arabia has plenty of cheap fuel, all the equipment needed to build and operate its plants has to be imported. It costs much more to build a plant there than it does in the United States, Europe, or Japan, which are the major markets for petrochemicals, aluminum, and steel. Because of the costs of operation, the distance to world markets, and competition for these products, the Saudi investment in these plants has not been very successful.

LOSING CONTROL OF WORLD OIL

Up until the 1980s, Saudi Arabia was able to control world oil prices. Since then, however, new oil discoveries in territories outside of OPEC member nations—in the North Sea, the Russian Arctic, and other parts of Africa—have led to fluctuations in the international price of oil. Because oil accounts for more than 80 percent of the Saudi economy, the country has had both good times and bad. So much has been spent on both modernizing the country and supporting the rich lifestyle of the members of the House of Saud that even the great oil incomes are not enough when the world price falls. Despite all of its oil money, Saudi Arabia today owes vast amounts to world banks.

NATURAL GAS

While oil is Saudi Arabia's largest revenue generator, the country has begun tapping into its vast natural gas resources. For decades, gas was a waste product that was burned off, creating light clearly visible from distant space. (Many of the "World at Night" maps show large clusters of light associated with a number of the world's major oil-producing areas.) Today, the value of gas as a clean-burning and relatively inexpensive economic resource is widely recognized.

The largest natural gas reserve is the Ghawar field, which extends from Saudi Arabia into the Persian Gulf, near the eastern coast towns of Safaniya and Zuluf. As the world's fourth-largest producer of natural gas, Saudi Arabia has immense potential to greatly increase its production and move up in the global rankings.

OTHER MINERALS

In addition to oil and natural gas, Saudi Arabia is endowed with abundant deposits of other minerals. Rich deposits of bauxite (the ore from which aluminum is made), copper, gold, and iron are mined and exported to neighboring nations. Because all mining operations are controlled by the Saudi government, the Saudi Arabian Mining Company was established in 1997 to oversee mineral extraction. The Mahd adh-Dhahab mine, located in the southwestern part of the country, is the largest gold mine. Historically, this area has been the most important mineral-producing region in the nation. Other gold deposits are located at Al-Hajar in the southeast and Ad-Duwaihi and Samran in the central regions of the nation. There also are zinc deposits in the northeastern mining town of Turaif and at Zargat in the southeastern region. Small deposits of these and other minerals are scattered throughout the country, particularly in the more remote areas, where production supports local economies.

EXPANDING AGRICULTURE

Nearly all crops in Saudi Arabia must be irrigated, and in the absence of surface freshwater supplies, this can be very costly. Historically, crop agriculture was limited to the few oasis sites scattered throughout the country, including the more humid mountainous area of the southwest. In this section of the book, however, our concern is with commercial, rather than folk subsistence, farming.

The chief generators of agricultural export revenue in Saudi Arabia are plantation products. For example, the nation's dates are some of the best in the world. Some of the most productive date plantations are located in the eastern provinces, particularly in Al Qatif and Al-Hasa. Fortunately, this area lies in close proximity to commercial markets in neighboring Kuwait, Qatar, and the United Arab Emirates. These Persian Gulf States also have well-developed seaports through which Saudi Arabian produce can be shipped abroad. Various types of fruit also are grown on plantations. Ample groundwater resources north of Riyadh, and the Buraydah and Unayzah regions, support some of the best fruit groves in the Middle East.

With the high cost of grain, meat, and dairy products, beginning in the 1970s, the House of Saud hoped to achieve self-sufficiency in the production of these foods. The Saudis particularly wanted to become self-sufficient in growing wheat, a staple of the Saudi diet. The government offered free land and loans for machinery, fertilizer, and seed, and a government guarantee to buy all the wheat produced at approximately 10 times the world price. Agriculture in the interior of the country depends entirely on irrigated water. Most is supplied by center-post sprinkler irrigation systems, in which a giant sprinkler sprays more than 1,000 gallons of a mixture of water and fertilizer each minute as it slowly moves in a circle around a center post. The wheat program was quite successful. In fact, in the 1980s, Saudi Arabia produced twice as much wheat as it needed. The government built grain elevators and storage silos to handle the surplus. With all the extra wheat, the government stopped the land-grant program and cut the guaranteed payment in half.

There have been agricultural programs and incentives designed to increase the production of other crops, as well. Saudi Arabia has invested heavily in hydroponics (growing plants in nutrient solutions, usually in greenhouses). In addition, production of vegetables such as tomatoes and cucumbers has increased. Other programs have improved the quality of sheep, cattle, and chickens and expanded dairy production.

TOURISM

Saudi Arabia has tremendous potential for the development of a very lucrative tourist industry. For a number of reasons, however, its development has been minimal. The problem is two-sided. First, few tourists are attracted to places where they are not wanted and where a tourist infrastructure (hotels,

Although tourism has not yet reached its full economic potential in Saudi Arabia, the economy does generate a sizeable amount of revenue from the annual hajj. In addition, sites such as Madain Saleh have become increasingly popular for foreign tourists. Located in northwestern Saudi Arabia, Madain Saleh was home to the Nabataeans, who controlled a vast trading network around present-day southern Jordan, Palestine, and northern Saudi Arabia.

restaurants and the availability of alcoholic beverages, rental car agencies, and other amenities travelers expect) has not been developed. Second, the Saudis remain highly suspicious of "foreigners," who, they fear, will "pollute their culture." A difficult question must be asked: When the oil is gone, where will the country turn for revenue?

The natural environment, history, and culture all present Saudi Arabia with at least three important features that could benefit tourism. Many tourists would find all three very attractive. During recent years, the tourist industry has shown some signs of growth, but this sector of the economy has barely scratched the surface of its ultimate potential. In particular, several coastal resorts along the Red Sea have attracted tourists from throughout Europe and the Middle East. Madain Saleh is a fascinating historical site located north of Medina. Once inhabited by the Nabatean Kingdom some 2,000 years ago, Madain Saleh is a visual treat filled with archeological wonders. The archeological remains in Madain are similar to the monolithic sculpture found in Petra, Jordan, and this is because Petra was the capital city of the Nabatean Kingdom. The growing interest of European visitors can also be seen in the newly constructed Movenpick resort on Al Nawras Island, off the coast near the city of Jiddah.

NEW CITIES, BIG CITIES

The most spectacular change in the modernization of Saudi Arabia has been the rise of the urban population. Before the discovery of oil, the only large cities were Jiddah, Mecca, and Medina. Riyadh was a tribal oasis town. Today, Riyadh, the capital and home of the House of Saud, is an enormous metropolitan area that is home to more than 4 million people. The Saudis have invested large sums of money to convert their traditional Arab towns into modern cities. Much of the new city designs depended on Western architects, planners, and engineers. Concrete and stucco buildings began to replace the adobe of the old Arab towns and villages. High-rise office buildings and apartment blocks similar to those in Western cities rose to the skies.

Recent urban growth has presented the country with a significant problem: transportation linkages. In the traditional folk culture, camels were the primary means of transportation. The transition from folk to contemporary urban culture has forced the country to play catch up with its transportation infrastructure, particularly its railways. Saudi Arabia does not have an integrated rail network. Currently, the major rail line in terms of traffic is the one linking the capital city, Riyadh, to the eastern port city of Ad Dammam. Other routes connect Riyadh to the city of Abu Ajram in the northwest and Al-Zabiva in the northeast. Surprisingly, no railway connects Riyadh with other major cities, including Jiddah and Mecca. Development of an integrated railway infrastructure is a key indicator of industrial growth. The future of economic development of Saudi Arabia—particularly as oil reserves begin to dwindle away—depends, at least in part, on the building of more railway lines linking the country's cities and regions.

PEOPLE: DEVELOPING THE COUNTRY'S GREATEST RESOURCE

Perhaps the most difficult resource for the House of Saud to develop has been the people of Saudi Arabia. The issue has been how best to bring them into the modern age. The government's first two five-year plans in the 1970s emphasized industrialization and the modernization of the economy. Since the 1980s, the emphasis has shifted to people and the development of human resources.

Top priorities are education, health, and social services. Modern school subjects were added to earlier Wahhabi religious training. In earlier days, the children of princes and merchants were sent to universities in the United States, the United Kingdom, or elsewhere in the West. Now, new Saudi universities have opened. Education has been extended to girls as well. Today, about 85 percent of Saudi men and 71 percent of the country's women are literate. Universal health care has resulted in fewer infant deaths. Life expectancy is now comparable to that in some European countries. There are almost 300 hospitals in the country, and the hospitals in Jiddah, Riyadh, and Ad Dammam are among the most modern and best-staffed in the world.

All these programs were designed to show that Saudi Arabia was the equal of any nation in the world. With so much money available, architects and engineers could easily turn dreams into reality. Modern style was in fashion, but with a distinctive Muslim-Arabian touch.

Perhaps the greatest hope for Saudi Arabia's future lies in the country's young people. In 2006, nearly 40 percent of the population was under 15 years of age, giving the country one of the world's youngest populations. Increasingly, young Saudis are channeling their energy into exploring—and being drawn into—the globalization phenomenon. A youthful population with a global vision will become increasingly impatient with many aspects of traditional culture and its values. This reality has caused a sharp divide in Saudi society along age lines.

Saudi society today is stratified into three broad groups. The elderly are still deeply imbedded in the values and ways of the traditional folk cultural system that promotes the old tribal kinship system and conservative religious values. Their children have witnessed the transition in the 1970s and 1980s, when the Saudi economy made its mark in the world scene, and thus constitute the hardworking middle class. The young are at the other end of the spectrum. They are exposed to the fast-changing world with modern innovations and rapidly developing contemporary popular culture. Amidst this whirlwind of cultural change, many young people are increasingly eager to embrace liberal values. In Saudi Arabia, the clash between "old" and "new" is greater than in many other culture realms.

Much of the growing frustration stems from the strict and inflexible Saudi society and its "rules." The unbendable Islamic Sharia law restricts their free movement, activity, social interactions, and freedom of expression in public places. For example, unmarried men are not allowed to enter shopping malls that are primarily intended for families and children. This is particularly frustrating to young adults when the neighboring nations of Bahrain and the United Arab Emirates are much more liberalized in accepting Western culture. They need only look to these and a number of other more liberal Muslim-dominated states to see people their own age who are much more in touch with popular contemporary culture. In Riyadh, however, there is some room for flexibility, and it is quite common to see young Saudis dressed in modern Western attire surfing the Internet in one of the many Internet cafes.

The future of Saudi Arabia is thus a mixture of often-conflicting strict Islamic laws controlled by the government and clergy and the vibrant energy of its youth. In recent years, there has been renewed pride among the youth. Following the 9/11 (2001) terrorist attacks on the United States and the involvement of 15 Saudi nationals in the horrific day, there has been a new emotional sentiment among the Saudi youth. Many young people are eager to showcase their country's rich history and culture and to prevent stereotyping of Saudi nationals as being terrorists.

7

Regions of Saudi Arabia

The large cities of Saudi Arabia are found in the three regions that contain most of the country's population: the Hejaz, along the northern two-thirds of the Red Sea coast; the Nadj in the center; and Al-Hasa in the east, near the Persian Gulf. Each region has a very different economy and is separated from the others by vast areas of nearly lifeless desert.

THE HEJAZ: THE LAND OF PILGRIMS

The Hejaz contains the holiest cities of Islam, Mecca and Medina, and the port-airport city of Jiddah, which serves as a gateway for millions of Muslim tourists each year. Saudi Arabia is proud that Mecca and Medina are the center of the vast Muslim world that stretches from Southeast Asia to the Atlantic Ocean and beyond to the Muslim communities in Europe and North America. The Saudis see it as their duty to protect Islam's holiest shrines and to provide Arab hospitality to the many pilgrims who make their personal hajj pilgrimages each year.

The result is that the two holy cities are entirely Islamic centers. Non-Muslims are not allowed in either Mecca or Medina. Each is surrounded by a series of checkpoints marked by pillars about 15 miles from the city, beyond which only devout Muslims are admitted.

The means of making the pilgrimage to Mecca and Medina have changed greatly over the years, but the ritual remains essentially the same. In the past, most pilgrims came by caravan along three main routes. From the west, one route crossed from Egypt across the narrow isthmus between the Red Sea and the Mediterranean, then went south, close to the Red Sea coast of Arabia. A second route from Turkey and the eastern Mediterranean came out of Damascus and Jerusalem, and crossed the western edge of the desert on the Arabian Peninsula. A third route from Iran and Baghdad followed oases across the center of Arabia. Pilgrim groups were highly organized under a commander, who had the power of a ship captain. The caravan had guides and soldiers to protect the party from Arab raiders. There were cooks, animal handlers, notaries, secretaries, physicians, and even a judge. Musicians played marching songs.

Getting to Mecca

With the coming of steamships and the building of the Suez Canal, pilgrims began to come by ship through the port of Jiddah. Today, some Bedouin pilgrims from throughout Arabia and the Middle East still come along the caravan routes, herding their sheep, goats, and camels as they travel. Ships still bring pilgrims through Jiddah. Many of the pilgrims, however, come by air through the new, modern airports at Jiddah and Riyadh. A whole terminal has been created for hajj pilgrims. Mecca itself has no airport. In fact, no airplanes are allowed to fly over the holy city. All pilgrims must travel the 50 miles from Jiddah to Mecca over land.

The port city of Jiddah, which is located on the Red Sea, is Saudi Arabia's second-largest city, behind Riyadh. Jiddah serves as the entry point for millions of Muslim tourists on their way to Mecca during the annual hajj.

Most of the 4 million annual pilgrims to Mecca come during the tenth month (Dhu'l) of the Muslim calendar, and usually between the eighth and seventeenth days of that month. Pilgrims can come at other times, but only for part of the rituals. Masses of people all gather to follow the same rituals. At times, there have been tragedies when people were killed after something caused the crowd to bolt.

In the center of the city is the sacred mosque of Mecca. Within it is a huge marble-floored courtyard to accommodate the crowds. In the center of the courtyard is the Ka'ba, a cube-shaped structure covered with a black cloth woven in Egypt that is taken down and replaced on the twenty-fifth day of Dhu'l each year. Pieces of the old cloth are sold to pilgrims as mementos of their hajj. The interior of the Ka'ba is empty except for pillars supporting the roof and a few gold and silver lamps hanging from the ceiling. In the eastern corner of the Ka'ba is the holy black stone that each pilgrim touches or kisses.

Mecca is more than a holy city. It is the bustling administrative center of a district of the country, with a population of around 1.3 million people. The Saudis have rebuilt much of the city, and there are apartment blocks and suburban homes as well as many hotels.

Medina: Birthplace of Islam

Many of the pilgrims to Mecca also proceed to Medina, 80 miles north of Mecca. It was there that the Prophet Muhammad first started a Muslim community. In fact, *Medina* means "prophet's city." Today, the site of Muhammad's tomb in the Prophet's Mosque is second only to the Ka'ba among sacred Muslim shrines. Muhammad himself helped build the mosque.

The city is in the midst of an oasis known for the production of dates and vegetables from irrigated fields. It has also been a center of pottery making. Although modern hotels and apartments and an Islamic university have been built here, much of old Medina remains. Medina, too, is the administrative center of its surrounding area and has a population approaching one million.

The Port of Jiddah and Other Cities

The city of Jiddah is far more than the entry point for hajj pilgrims. Since foreign embassies earlier were prohibited in Riyadh, Jiddah is the center of the diplomatic community of Saudi Arabia. It is also the closest port to Europe and North America, so many imports pass through the port, then move by road to Riyadh. Jiddah also has one of the largest desalination plants in the world and an oil refinery that primarily serves its needs and those of Mecca. In many respects, Jiddah is Saudi Arabia's "window to the world," as well as being the country's second-largest urban center with a population of nearly 3.5 million.

The other important cities of the Hcjaz are Ta'if in the highlands above Mecca, and Yambu, the oil-shipping port at the end of the pipeline from the oil fields in the east. Many of Mecca's workers live in Ta'if. Yambu is home to two oil refineries and a modern tanker facility.

THE NADJ

This is the traditional heartland of Arabia: the land of the Bedouin and the oasis farmer. It is also homeland of the House of Saud. Ibn Saud made Riyadh his capital and the most important city in the country. It remains the residence of the most senior princes of the House of Saud. It is also the country's center of government. Herc are the headquarters of most of the government agencies that oversee the country's economic development and social programs. As the largest (with about 5.5 million people in the metropolitan area) and richest of all Saudi cities, it has become a great marketplace of shops and stores. It has the finest university and hospitals in the country. With a majority of the country's motor vehicles, Riyadh has a refinery to serve its needs and those of other parts of the interior. Many of the country's largest private businesses and richest business families also are based in the booming capital city.

Riyadh is the focus of roads from other parts of the country and a railroad connects it with Ad Dammam, the oil center on the Persian Gulf. Riyadh's airport is a measure of its connections with the rest of the country and the world. Although foreign embassies have been prohibited in the city, Riyadh is where the leaders of world governments and

The capital and largest city of Saudi Arabia, Riyadh is home to more than 4 million people, which is approximately 20 percent of the nation's population. Although it is located in an arid region, Riyadh's name means "place of garden and trees" in Arabic.

businesses come to meet with the House of Saud and the government. The city's modern airport is busy with the coming and going of government and business leaders. Many foreign workers also travel through it, as do some of the pilgrims to Mecca. Riyadh's population has sprawled out into the desert, beyond the city limits. There, suburbs have been built. Other oasis towns are also connected to Riyadh by modern roads. Buraydah and Unayzah, more than 100 miles (160 kilometers) away from Riyadh, are cities with populations approaching 100,000. They are part of a series of oases settlements that extend along either side of the northwest-southeast ridges in the center of the country.

The central location of Riyadh and its historical importance as a key city in the Arab world was recently recognized by the United Nations Educational, Scientific and Cultural Organization (UNESCO). In 2000, the body named Riyadh as the "Cultural capital of the Arab world." Over the years, Riyadh has been in the crossroads of Arab and Islamic cultural change. For instance, before the Prophet Muhammad, oral traditions and poetry were widespread among the predominant Bedouins in the Nadj and Riyadh. Following the birth of Islam and use of written communication, Riyadh became a key center for written communication. As a result, an era of Islamic literature emerged in Riyadh that continues even today.

The city is not only a key administrative center and the capital city of Saudi Arabia, but is also home to several important cultural events promoted by Islamic institutions. For instance, evening gatherings, or *majlis*, follow the day's last prayer. This is a hallmark cultural trait within the Islamic cultural system in Saudi Arabia and other Muslim nations. In recent times, the desert tradition of Bedouins has blended with modernity to prompt majli gatherers of Riyadh to hold elaborate evening get-togethers in modern-styled tents with generous servings of the best Arabic food.

AL-HASA

The region along the Persian Gulf has the third-largest population concentration in Saudi Arabia. In the middle of the twentieth century, the area was sparsely populated. There were only a few tiny ports along the Persian Gulf and some oases settlements back from the coast. Bedouins roamed most of the land in search of grazing land for their animals.

Today, Al-Hasa is the most important part of Saudi Arabia's economy. It is there that most of the country's oil is produced. All of Al-Hasa's major cities have been built as part of the oil industry. They are centers of well-drilling, pipelines, and refineries, and some are oil-shipping ports. These cities, which also house much of the population of foreign workers, are where the North Americans and Europeans and other foreign laborers take care of the various oil-field operations.

The largest city is Ad Dammam, one of the world's most modern ports. It has a metropolitan area population of around 1.6 million people. It was the site of an old port where small sailing ships traded with camel caravans along the trade route from India and Southeast Asia to the Middle East and the Mediterranean Sea. The remains of an old castle lie atop a coral reef close to shore. However, the harbor was insufficient for modern ships, so a new, modern port had to be built. That port stretches for more than seven miles along the coast.

Ad Dammam is more than an oil port. It is the chief Saudi port on the Persian Gulf. It not only receives most of the equipment and supplies needed for oil operations, but, with railroad connection to Riyadh, the city is also the receiving port for the country's capital.

Part of the urban complex of Ad Dammam is the city of Dhahran, the site of the country's first oil well in 1934. Dhahran was a desert in those days, but it soon became the site for the headquarters of all ARAMCO oil operations.

The first oil prospectors in Saudi Arabia landed at the small port of Jubail. At that time, Jubail was the base for a pearl-fishing fleet. It had the deepest harbor on the Persian Gulf, and handled cargoes for traders who managed camel caravans to Riyadh and other oases in the interior. Today, Jubail is the site of one of the largest industrial developments in Saudi Arabia. In addition to an oil refinery, there are petrochemical plants, a steel mill, and an aluminum plant. The new port can handle large global freighters and tankers.

THREE SEPARATE REGIONS, VERY DIFFERENT IN CHARACTER

The location of the three population centers along the Red Sea coast in the west, around Riyadh in the center of the country, and in the oil fields of the northeast presents Saudi Arabia with great transportation and communications problems. Even today, Jiddah has no rail connection with the other two centers of population. Ad Dammam and Riyadh are linked by rail, but surface transport links are expensive to build and difficult to maintain in the severe desert environment. The easiest connections between the three population centers of the country are by air.

Each of the three population centers is also very different culturally. Life in Jiddah, Mecca, and Medina is focused on taking care of pilgrims to the holy city. There, the people are more concerned about the global extent of Islam than about Saudi Arabia itself.

At the other extreme, in the oil fields of the northeast, there is a very different international face to Saudi Arabia. If the west is the religious heart of worldwide Islam, the northeast is a secular world centered on producing and exporting oil and gas. This region is mostly populated by non-Saudis, and its output is geared to the technology and the markets of North America, Europe, and Japan. Production rises and falls with the price and demand for world oil. Foreign workers, rather than native Saudis, form the largest share of its population. The Saudis want to ease into the cosmopolitan international lifestyle that comes from Western industrial countries, but on their own terms. They do not want to be forced into change by the many foreigners living temporarily in their country.

The heart of Saudi life is the Nadj, in the center of the country. This is where the Bedouin-Wahhabi tradition began and where it remains strong. Most of all, this is the home of the House of Saud and the capital city of Riyadh.

Governing the three very different population centers of Saudi Arabia is not easy. Even harder is balancing the strong traditions of Wahhabi Islam and the values of the modern global lifestyle. The House of Saud has managed to do this over the years, but not without problems. The religious Saudi conservatives do not like change. They consider many of the new ways an attack on their religion. Moreover, Bedouins are not interested in participating as workers in the modern economy. The routine of daily office or factory hours is completely different from the nomadic life to which they are accustomed.

8

Saudi Arabia Looks Ahead

The future of Saudi Arabia is unclear. As in the recent past, everything depends on oil. It is the one major product that the country contributes to the global economy. The Saudis have had only limited success trying to develop other industries based on oil. Despite the limitations of the Saudi economy, there is still enough oil for Saudi Arabia to maintain its position as the world's largest producer for an estimated 100 years.

Some observers, however, wonder if Saudi Arabia and the House of Saud will be able to continue to control their oil. The nation's neighbor, Iraq, has already tried to take control of the country of Kuwait and its oil production. It is possible that trouble in the Middle East between the Muslims and Jews over Israel will draw Saudi Arabia into war.

ARAB POLITICS

Tensions in the Middle East are a major concern for Saudi Arabia. Formation of the Jewish state of Israel in Palestine in 1948 created problems for Saudi Arabia and the rest of the Muslim world. Palestinian Arabs, most of them Muslims, fled as Jewish settlers occupied the lands on which the Arabs had lived for centuries. Many of the refugees have lived in refugee camps in the surrounding Arab countries ever since. Most Arab countries have not recognized the legitimacy of the state of Israel.

As the richest Arab country and the site of the holy cities of Islam, Saudi Arabia has strongly opposed Israel. However, the United States, Israel's chief supplier of money and military equipment, is Saudi Arabia's main oil market. This makes for a tricky political situation at times, as Saudi Arabia develops its policies for well into the twenty-first century.

What about Saudi Arabia itself? Will the House of Saud be able to control the often opposing forces of modernization and tradition? Will the young technocrats and other professionals continue to accept their second-tier position in their country? Will the Wahhabi fundamentalists rebel against the replacement of their values with modern ideas? Will the Saudis continue to depend on foreign workers—engineers, architects, and economists—to run their economy, and to do the jobs Saudis do not want to do?

Perhaps the biggest question of all is what the future holds for oil. In the past, the demand for oil and its price have gone sharply up and down each year. It is hard for a country to make plans when it cannot know what its income will be from one year to the next.

The biggest uncertainty in regard to oil, however, is whether the world will continue to have such a huge demand for it. Already, alternative sources of energy, such as hydrogen, fuel cells, ethanol and bio-diesel, and both wind and solar power, are being developed. If the world made a major shift to any of them, Saudi

Although Western influences have made their way into Saudi Arabian culture, Wahhabi fundamentalists still largely dictate what most women wear in public. For example, students at the Hekma College for Women in Jiddah are required to wear an abaya in public and in the presence of their close male family members.

Arabia's global importance and wealth would diminish rapidly. It seems that the future of oil, the commodity that started it all, and that guarantees Saudi influence, is in doubt. Powerful tensions have also arisen between the new ways of industrialization and the honored Bedouin and Islamic traditions on which the country was founded. Saudi Arabia has become a world power, but its strength is threatened by dangerous instabilities.

SAUDI ARABIA AND THE WAR ON TERRORISM

In some respects, the future of Saudi Arabia may rely on its role in keeping a check on the worldwide war on terrorism. Its strategic geopolitical position is based on both its central location within the Islamic world and also the vital role the country plays in bridging the Islamic and Western worlds, with its oil being the key bargaining chip. Immediately after the 9/11/2001 terrorist attacks on the United States, the international community began to look to Saudi Arabia for leadership. As the spiritual center of Islam, many people look to Saudi Arabia in the hope that it can help to prevent further acts of terrorism involving Islamic fundamentalists. As was noted previously, the key participants in the 9/11 terrorist attacks were Saudi nationals, including the leader of al-Qaeda, Osama Bin Laden. The kingdom nation understands its unique role and has taken several steps to counter terrorism. The people of Saudi Arabia have come face-to-face with terrorism. In 2003, a series of bomb explosions ripped through the capital city of Riyadh killing 90 people and injuring 160. The House of Saud has taken strict measures in combating terrorism since 9/11.

HOLDING THE MIDDLE EAST TOGETHER

As the world's leading producer of oil and its key role as the center of Islam, Saudi Arabia holds a very strong position of global importance. The kingdom nation has its own share of internal problems with Islamic extremists. Sunni Muslim terrorists have aligned themselves with their chief promoter, al-Qaeda, to bring down the moderate Saudi government. In recent years, these internal conflicts have worsened. The 2003 Riyadh bombings were followed by the 2004 Yanbu attacks, and in 2006, a major attack was prevented at the Abqaiq refinery on the oil-rich eastern Saudi coast. In another war front, Saudi Arabia has offered to assist the United States in helping the Sunni nationals in the war in Iraq. Saudi Arabia, along with Egypt, ranks among the region's strongest allies of the United

Many Western nations look to Saudi Arabia to serve as a pillar of the Muslim world in the fight against terrorism. The future of relations between Muslim countries and the West may well fall on the shoulders of Saudi Arabia's youth.

States in the quest to bring lasting peace to the troubled Middle East. The future of Saudi Arabia is crucial with respect to maintaining the balance between its Islamic commitments to neighboring nations and helping the West in the War on Terrorism. The recent reforms made by King Abdullah in strongly cracking down on terror suspects are seen as a positive sign.

In conclusion, few countries can match Saudi Arabia's potential. It has vast mineral wealth, historic treasures, and is the spiritual center of the world's second-largest and fastest-growing religion. It has a young and increasingly well-educated population, a population with rapidly rising expectations. Yet Saudi Arabia faces a critical dilemma; the country is trapped between a very conservative, traditional way of life and the realities of twenty-first-century globalization. Saudi Arabia's future really hinges on how well the country and its 27 million citizens are able to make this difficult transition.

Physical Geography

Location Middle East, bordering the Persian Gulf and the Red Sea, north of Yemen

Area 830,000 square miles (2,149,690 square kilometers)

Boundaries Total: 4,431 kilometers; Border countries: Iraq, 506 miles (814 kilometers); Jordan, 462 miles (744 kilometers); Kuwait, 138 miles (222 kilometers); Oman, 420 miles (676 kilometers); Qatar, 37 miles (60 kilometers); UAE, 284 miles (457 kilometers); Yemen, 906 miles (1,458 kilometers)

Coastlines 1,639 miles (2,640 kilometers), on Red Sea, the Persian Gulf, and the Arabian Sea

Climate Harsh, dry desert with great temperature extremes

Terrain Mostly uninhabited, sandy desert

Elevation Extremes Lowest point is Persian Gulf, sea level; highest point is Jabal Sawda', 10,279 feet (3,133 meters) above sea level

Land Use Arable land, 1.67%; permanent crops, 0.09%; other, 98.24% (2005)

Irrigated Land 6,253 square miles (16,200 square kilometers) (2003)

Natural Hazards Frequent sand and dust storms

Natural Resources Petroleum, natural gas, iron ore, gold, copper

Environmental Issues Desertification; depletion of underground water resources; the lack of perennial rivers or permanent water bodies has prompted the development of extensive seawater desalination facilities; coastal pollution from oil spills

People

Population 27,601,038 (2007); males, 15,034,806 (2007 est.); females, 12,566,232 (2007 est.)

Population Density 8 people per square mile (11 people per square kilometer)

Population Growth Rate 2.06% (2007 est.)

Net Migration Rate -5.95 migrant(s)/1,000 population (2007 est.)

Fertility Rate 3.94 children born/woman (2007 est.)

Birthrate 29.1 births per 1,000 population (2007)

Death Rate 2.55 deaths per 1,000 population (2007)

Life Expectancy at Birth	Total population: 75.8 years; male, 73.9 years; female, 78.0 years (2007 est.)
Median Age	total: 21.4; male, 22.9; female, 19.6 (2007 est.)
Ethnic Groups	Arab, 90%, Afro-Asian, 10%
Religion	Muslim, 100%
Language	Arabic (official)
Literacy	(Age 15 and over can read and write) Total population: 78.8% (84.7%, male; 70.8%, female) (2003)

Economy

Currency	Saudi riyal (SAR)
GDP Purchasing Power Parity	(PPP) $366 billion (2006 est.)
GDP Per Capita	$13,600 (2006 est.)
Labor Force	7.125 million *note*: more than 35% of the population in the 15–64 age group is nonnational (2006 est.)
Unemployment	13% among Saudi males only (local bank estimate; some estimates range as high as 25%) (2004 est.)
Labor Force by Occupation	Services, 63%; industry, 25%; agriculture, 12%
Agricultural Products	Wheat, barley, tomatoes, melons, dates, citrus; mutton, chickens, eggs, milk
Industries	Crude oil production, petroleum refining, basic petrochemicals; ammonia, industrial gases, sodium hydroxide (caustic soda), cement, fertilizer, plastics; metals, commercial ship repair, commercial aircraft repair, construction
Exports	$204.5 billion f.o.b. (2006 est.)
Imports	$64.16 billion f.o.b. (2006 est.)
Leading Trade Partners	Exports: Japan, 17.6%; U.S., 15.8%; South Korea, 9.6%; China, 7.2%; Singapore, 4.4%; Taiwan, 4.4% (2006) Imports: U.S., 12.2%; Germany, 8.5%; China, 7.9%; Japan, 7.2%; UK, 4.8% (2005)
Export Commodities	Petroleum and petroleum products, 90%
Import Commodities	Machinery and equipment, foodstuffs, chemicals, motor vehicles, textiles
Transportation	Roadways: 94,476 miles (152,044 kilometers), 28,248 miles (45,461 kilometers) is paved (2004); Railways:

865 miles (1,392 kilometers); Airports: 208–73 are paved runways (2006)

Government

Country Name	Conventional long form: Kingdom of Saudi Arabia; conventional short form: Saudi Arabia; local long form: Al Mamlakah al Arabiyah as Suudiyah; local short form: Al Arabiyah as Suudiyah
Capital City	Riyadh
Type of Government	Monarchy
Head of Government	King and Prime Minister Abdullah bin Abdul Aziz Al Saud (Since August 1, 2005)
Independence	September 23, 1932 (unification of the kingdom)
Administrative Divisions	13 provinces (mintaqat, singular–mintaqah)

Communications

TV Stations	117 (1997)
Radio Stations	74 (AM, 43; FM, 31)
Phones	17,500,000 (including 13,300,000 cell phones)
Internet Users	3.2 million (2006)

* Source: *CIA-The World Factbook* (2007)

A.D. 570	Birth of Muhammad.
622	Muhammad flees Mecca (beginning of the Muslim calendar).
624	Muhammad captures Mecca.
632	Muhammad dies.
Late 1700s	The religious reforms of Muhammad bin abd al-Wahhab in Arabia; Saud family becomes the protector of Wahhabism in the Nadj.
1880	Birth of Ibn Saud.
1891	Saud family flees Riyadh and takes refuge in Kuwait.
1902	Ibn Saud recaptures Riyadh and begins consolidation of the Nadj and most of Arabia.
1923	Ibn Saud agrees to first oil concession, but nothing comes of it.
1924	Saudis capture the Hadiz and Mecca.
1932	Ibn Saud establishes Saudi Arabia.
1933	Oil concession granted to Standard Oil of California (SOCO).
1936	First productive oil well.
1939–1945	World War II causes oil production to cease, but exploration continues.
1944	ARAMCO formed between SOCO and Texaco.
1948	Esso and Socony Vacuum become members of ARAMCO.
1953	Death of Ibn Saud; his son Saud bin Abdul Aziz becomes king.
1962	Organization of Petroleum Exporting Countries (OPEC) formed with Iran, Iraq, Kuwait, Saudi Arabia, and Venezuela as charter members.
1966	Faisal bin Abdul Aziz becomes king.
1970	First of five five-year development plans for the country begins.
1971	Saudi embargo on oil shipments to the United States.
1975	Faisal assassinated; brother Khalid bin Abdul Aziz becomes king.
1980	Saudi government takes over ARAMCO.
1982	Fahd bin Abdul Aziz becomes king.
1991	Persian Gulf War against Iraq.
1993	King Fahd issues a decree for creation of 13 new administrative divisions in Saudi Arabia.

1994	Dissident Osama Bin Laden is stripped of his Saudi Arabian citizenship.
1999	For the first time in Saudi history, women attend a government session.
2001	Fifteen of the 19 hijackers involved in the 9/11 terrorist attacks on United States are Saudi nationals.
2003	A major dissident rally by more than 300 Saudi intellectuals demanding democracy leads to police breakdown and arrests; terrorist attacks perpetrated by the fundamentalist group al-Qaeda in Riyadh kills 90 and injures 160.
2005	The first ever Saudi Arabian municipal elections are conducted; women are not allowed to vote; King Fahd passes away; his half brother Crown Prince Abdullah Bin-Abd-al-Aziz Al Saud takes over as the new king of Saudi Arabia; World Trade Organization invites Saudi Arabia after more than 12 years of negotiations.
2006	Saudi Arabian government thwarts a major suicide bomb attack linked to al-Qaeda.

Glossary

Ad Dahna: River of sand that separates Nadj from al Hasis Al-Hasa in Eastern Saudi Arabia; the major oil-producing area and oil shipping ports along the Persian Gulf.

Ad Dammam: Largest city of Eastern Saudi Arabia; headquarters of oil operations.

Allah: God of Islam.

aquifer: Underground source of water.

Arabs: Culture group in the Middle East and North Africa whose members speak Arabic; Arabs include people of the Arabian Peninsula, Iraqis, Syrians, Jordanians, the majority in Lebanon, Palestinians, and Egyptians.

ARAMCO: The Arabian American Oil Company, established by Standard Oil of California, New Jersey, and New York, and Texaco to produce and ship oil produced in Saudi Arabia; taken over by Saudi government in 1982.

Azir: Southwestern part of the country.

Bedouins: Desert nomad tribes and related townspeople.

Bin: Means "son of," also written "ibn."

Dammam Dome: First Saudi oil field developed; site of the city of Ad Dammam.

dromedary: One-humped, short-haired camel of Arabia.

Empty Quarter: Vast, almost unpopulated desert of the south.

Great Nafud: Desert area that separates northern Arabia from Nadj and the Hejaz.

hajj: The pilgrimage to Mecca.

Hejaz: Northwestern Saudi Arabia, where the holy cities of Mecca and Medina are located, along with the major port city Jiddah.

House of Saud: Members of the ruling Saud family, descendants of Ibn Saud.

Ibn Saud (Abdul Aziz Al Saud): Founder of Saudi Arabia and its first king; father of all kings since.

Islam: The religion proclaimed by the Prophet Muhammad; the state religion of Saudi Arabia.

Jiddah: Major port of Saudi Arabia; center of business in Hadiz; point of entry for pilgrims to Mecca.

Ka'ba: The holy stone in the great mosque of Mecca thought to date back to Adam and Eve.

Koran (*Qur'an*): Holy book of Islam; considered the constitution of Saudi Arabia.

Mecca: The holiest city of Islam; devout Muslims pray five times a day facing Mecca.

Medina: Second-holiest city of Islam, where the Prophet Muhammad is buried.

mosque: Holy place of worship for Muslims.

Muslim: Follower of the Islamic religion.

Nadj: Central part of the country; traditional home of the House of Saud; includes Riyadh, the country's capital.

oasis: Settlement around a water source in the desert.

OPEC: Organization of Petroleum Exporting Countries, formed in 1962; current members: Algeria, Angola, Indonesia, Iran, Iraq, Kuwait, Libya, Nigeria, Qatar, Saudi Arabia, United Arab Emirates, and Venezuela.

Ramadan: Holy month in the Muslim calendar when Muslims fast from dawn to sundown.

Riyadh: Traditional home of the House of Saud; capital and the largest city of Saudi Arabia.

Sharia: Islamic law that controls government, law, and all aspects of the Saudi culture.

sheik: Chieftain of a Bedouin tribe.

wadi: Stream valley in the desert that is dry most of the time but often floods after rainfall.

Wahhabi: Follower of Muhammad bin Abd al-Wahhab, an eighteenth-century Islamic leader who preached the return to the values of the Prophet Muhammad's day; Wahhabism is very traditional and antimodern.

Yambu: Oil and natural gas shipping port on the Red Sea.

Bibliography

al-Rasheed, Madawi. *A History of Saudi Arabia.* Cambridge, U.K.: Cambridge University Press, 2002.

Barfield, Thomas. *The Nomadic Alternative.* Englewood Cliffs, N.J.: Prentice Hall, 1993.

Central Intelligence Agency. *Issues in the Middle East Atlas,* 1973.

Foud al-Farsey. *Modernity and Tradition: The Saudi Equation.* New York: Kegan Paul International, 1990.

International Energy Agency. *Middle East Oil and Gas,* 1995.

Janin, Hunt, and Margaret Besheer. *Saudi Arabia.* New York: Benchmark Books, 2003.

Kaplan, Robert. *The Arabists.* New York: The Free Press, 1995.

Lacey, Robert. *The Kingdom: Arabia and the House of Sa'ud.* New York: Harcourt Brace Jovanovich, 1981.

Life World Library. *The Arab World.* New York: Time, 1962.

Long, David. *Culture and Customs of Saudi Arabia.* Westport, Conn.: Greenwood Press, 2005.

Mackay, Sandra. *The Saudis: Inside the Desert Kingdom.* New York: W. W. Norton, 2002.

———. *The Saudis.* Boston: Houghton Mifflin, 1987.

Nawwab Ismail, Peter Speers, and Paul Hoye. *ARAMCO and Its World: Arabia and the Middle East.* Dhaahran: ARAMCO, 1981.

The Times Atlas of World History (revised edition). Maplewood, N.J.: Hammond, 1984.

World Almanac and Book of Facts 2002. New York: World Almanac Books, 2001.

World Satellite Atlas of the World. Toronto: Warwick Publishing, 1997.

Books

Gritzner, Jeffrey A., and Charles F. Gritzner. *North Africa and the Middle East.* New York: Chelsea House, 2006.

Kheirabadi, Masoud. *Islam.* New York: Chelsea House, 2004.

Reed, Jennifer Bond. *The Saudi Royal Family.* New York: Chelsea House, 2007.

Wagner, Heather Lehr. *Saudi Arabia* (Creation of the Modern Middle East). New York: Chelsea House, 2002.

Wynbrandt, James. *A Brief History of Saudi Arabia.* New York: Facts On File, 2004.

Web sites

Economist Magazine: Saudi Arabia
www.economist.com/countries/saudiarabia/

Library of Congress: Saudi Arabia
www.lcweb2.loc.gov/frd/cs/satoc.html

The Middle East Institute: Saudi Arabia
http://www.mideasti.org/countries/countries.php?name= saudi percent20arabia

BBC Country Profile: Saudi Arabia
http://news.bbc.co.uk/2/hi/middle_east/country_profiles/791936.stm

The Royal Embassy of Saudi Arabia in Washington, D.C.
http://www.saudiembassy.net/Country/Country.asp

U.S. State Department: Saudi Arabia
www.state.gov/r/pa/ei/bgr/3584.htm

Picture Credits

Abdul Aziz, 11, 13, 61–62, 64, 76
Abdul Aziz, Saud bin, 61
Abdullah bin Abdul Aziz Al Saud
    (King Abdullah), 65–67
Abqaiq refinery, 102
Ad Dahna, 28
Ad Dammam, 46–47, 72, 93, 96
Ad-Duwaihi, 82
agriculture, 21–22, 26, 41–43,
    82–83
airports, 90, 93–94
Al Qatif, 82
alcohol, 14, 57
Al-Hajar, 82
Al-Hasa, 29–30, 82, 95–96
Allah, 12, 49–50
al-Noor Mountain, 25
al-Qatif, 70
Al-Sayadiah, 57
alternative fuels, 100–101
aluminum, 82, 96
Aqaba, Gulf of, 23
aquifers, 42–43
Ar Rub al-Khali (Empty Quarter), 22,
    24, 31–32
Arabian American Oil Company
    (ARAMCO), 71–72, 74–75, 96
Arabian horses, 39
Arabian Peninsula, 12, 20–23
Arabian Sea, Azir and, 26
Arabic language, 12, 53
arable land, lack of, 21, 22
archeology, 85
Asir Mountains, 41
Azir, 26

Bahrain, 20, 69, 88
bauxite, 82
Bedouins
    Arab culture and, 13
    coffee and, 58
    history of, 47–49
    impact of oil on, 78–79
    Nadj and, 26, 28
    overview of, 35–36, 38–41

pilgrimages and, 19
    return to lifestyle of, 59–60
Buraydah, 94–95

calendars, 50
camels, 13, 19, 36–38
capital punishment, 14
cardamom, 57–58
climate, 21–23, 32–34
coffee, 26, 57–58
Commission for Promotion of Virtue
    and Vice, 65
conservatism, Islamic principles and, 13
construction, 70–71, 77–78
Council of Ministers, 63
crops. See agriculture
culture, 40–41, 95, 97

Dammam Dome, 69–70
Damran, 82
dates, 42, 58, 82
Dead Sea, 23
desalination plants, 43, 92–93
deserts, 21, 22–23
Dhu al-Hijja, 48, 53
Dhu'l, 91–92
dress, traditional, 40
drilling, 69, 96
driving, women and, 56
dromedary camels, 36, 37–38
drug use, 14

economy. See also oil
    agriculture and, 82–83
    broadening of, 80–81
    minerals and, 82
    modernization and, 85–86
    natural gas and, 81
    people and, 86–88
    tourism and, 83–85
    women and, 56
Eden, Garden of, 26
education, 56, 78, 80, 86
elections, 55, 67
Empty Quarter, 22, 24, 31–32

Index

escorts, need for, 56
Ethiopia, 23, 57
Eurasian Plate, 23
Exxon, 71

fasting, 50
flash flooding, 32
food, overview of, 56–57
foreign workers
    construction and, 77
    control of, 78
    increasing numbers of, 73
    isolation of, 65
    Jiddah and, 92
    Riyadh and, 93–94
    role of, 97
    temporary nature of, 79–80
fruit, 82–83
fuels, alternative, 100–101
future of Saudi Arabia, 99–104

Garden of Eden, 26
gawha, 57–58
Ghawar natural gas field, 81
Gobi Desert, 22
gold, 82
government, Nadj and, 93
grazing, Azir and, 26
Great Depression, 69
Great Nafud, 28
groundwater, 42–43

hadith, 13, 52–53
Ha'il, 29
harisah, 57
health care, 86
Hejaz, 24–26, 89–93
    cuisine of, 57
horses, 39
hospitals, 86
House of Saud
    Islam and, 12
    Koran and, 52
    leadership of country and, 62–63

mineral rights and, 74
Nadj and, 28–29, 93
overview of, 61–62
humidity, 33
hydroponics, 83

Ibn Saud, Abdul Iziz, 11, 13, 61–62,
    64, 76
icebergs, 43
ijma, Sharia law and, 13
infrastructure, oil production and,
    72–73
interior region. See Nadj
Iran, oil and, 17, 68–69, 73
Iraq, 17, 30
irrigation, 41–42, 83
Islam. See also Muslims; Wahhabi sect
    of Islam
    calendar of, 50
    diversity within, 65–66
    foreign workers and, 78
    Mecca, Medina and, 89–93
    Muhammad and, 50–51, 52–53
    overview of, 49–50
    Saudi Arabia as center of, 12
    spread of, 51–52
    terrorism and, 102
Israel, 23, 100

Jabal Sawda', 21, 23
Jabal Shammar Mountains, 29
Jabal Tuwayq, 28
Jiddah, 18, 25, 46–47, 56, 92–93
jihad, 65
Jordan, 30
Jordan River, 23
Jubail, 96
jubniyyah, 57

Ka'ba, 48, 49, 53, 91–92
kings, role of, 62–63, 64
Koran, 12, 13, 52–53
kubez bread, 57
Kuwait, 20, 29, 72, 82

lahuh, 57
language, 12, 53

Madain Saleh, 84, 85
Mahd adh-Dhahab mine, 82
majlis, 64, 95
maps of Saudi Arabia, 10, 21
Maskid Al-Haram Mosque, 48
Mecca
    as capital of Hejaz, 25
    Ibn Saud and, 62
    importance of, 49
    Muhammad and, 12, 51
    pilgrimages and, 48
    population density and, 46–47
    prayer and, 17, 18, 53–55
    traveling to, 90–92
Medina
    Ibn Saud and, 62
    Islam and, 90, 92
    Muhammad and, 12, 50, 51
    population density and, 46–47
    trade and, 25
Mesopotamia, 30
mineral resources, 74, 81, 82. See also oil
Mobil, 71
modernization
    Bedouins and, 39–40
    as difficult balance, 16–17
    effect of, 64–65
    impact of oil on, 76–80, 85–86
Mogul tribesmen, 52
mosques, 17, 48, 53–54, 91
Mozambique, 23
Muhammad, 12, 13, 49–51, 92
Muslims, 12. See also Islam
mustahaab, 53
Mutawa'een, 56

Nabataean Kingdom, 84, 85
Nadj, 27–29, 93–95, 97
Nafud, Great, 28
Namira Mosque, 53–54
natural gas, 81

Nayef (Prince), 65
neutral zone, 29
nomads. See Bedouins
Northwest region. See Hejaz

oasis areas, 28, 92
ocean water, desalination of, 43
oil
    Al-Hasa and, 29, 30, 96
    broadening of economy and, 80–81
    construction and, 72–73, 77–78
    control of production of, 74–75
    current production of, 72
    drilling permission and, 69
    effect of discovery of, 8–9
    exploration and, 69–71
    foreign workers and, 78
    future of Saudi Arabia and, 99–100
    global importance of, 14–15
    impact of on society, 78–80
    importance of to economy, 68–69,
        75–77
    increased production of, 71–72
    loss of control of world market
        and, 81
    natural gas and, 81
    shipping of in Persian Gulf, 73–74
Oman, 20
OPEC, 75, 81
Osama bin Laden, 16, 102

pagan gods, 49–50
Palestine, 100
Persian Gulf, 22, 29–30, 73–74
Persian Gulf War, 16
petrochemicals, 80, 96
pilgrimages
    Bedouins and, 19
    Hejaz and, 89–93
    Mecca and, 12, 48, 53–55
pipelines, 73–74, 93
politics, 65–66, 100–101
population, location of majority of, 22,
        46–47, 89, 97–98

Index

pork, 57
ports, 96
prayer, modernization and, 16–17, 18
precipitation, 22, 26, 32–33, 41–42
property rights, 56, 80
prophets, 12, 49–50

Qatar, 20
qiyas, 14
Qur'an, 12, 13, 52–53

railroads, 86, 97
rainfall, 22
Ramadan, 50
Ras Tanura, 71, 73
Red Sea, 22, 23, 26, 46
refineries, 75, 80, 93, 96, 102
reform, King Abdullah and, 67
rice, 57
rifts, 23
"river of sand," 28
Riyadh
    aquifers and, 43
    as capital, 22
    description of, 76
    growth of, 85, 93–95
    Ibn Saud and, 62
    population density and, 46–47
    terrorism in, 102
    women and, 56
royalties, 69, 74

Sahara Desert, 22
sand, camels and, 38
Saud, Abdullah bin Abdul Aziz Al-,
        65–67
Saudi Arabian Airlines, 18
Saudi Peace Plan of King Abdullah, 67
seafood, 57
segregation, foreign workers and, 78
Semites, 47
September 11 attacks, 16, 88, 102
Sharia law, 13, 43–44, 55–56, 87–88
sharifs, 60
Shaybah oil field, 15

sheiks, 36
shepherds, 39
Shia Muslims, 66
shipping, oil and, 73
Shura Council, 67
slavery, 76
society, stratification of, 87–88
Socony-Vacuum, 71
southwest region. See Azir
Standard Oil Company (SOCO), 14, 71
stratification of, of society, 87–88
Sunnah, 53
Sunni Muslims, 13, 102

Ta'if, 93
Taqarub Islam, 65–66
Tawhid school of Islam, 65
temperature, extremes in, 34
terraces, agriculture and, 26
terrorism, 16, 88, 102
Texaco, 71
Tihama, 26
tourism, 83–85, 91
trade, Hejaz and, 25–26
tradition, Islamic principles and, 13
Trans-Arabian Pipeline (TAP), 73
transportation, 86
Tropic of Cancer, 33

ulemas, 53, 63
Unayzah, 94–95
UNESCO, 95
United Arab Emirates, 20, 88
United States, oil and, 17–18

voting rights, 55, 67

Wadi as Sirhan, 30
wadis, 24–25, 32
Wahhab, Muhammad ibn-Abd al-,
        60, 65
Wahhabi sect of Islam
    discontent with, 63
    modernization and, 16–17
    strict nature of, 13, 60

Tawhid school of Islam and, 65
    women and, 101
wajib, 53
wastewater management, 44–45
water
    aquifers and, 42–43
    camels and, 36–38
    importance of, 34, 41–42
    Jabal Tuwayq and, 28
    laws concerning, 43–44
    wastewater management and, 44–45
water table, lowering of, 43
welfare states, 64–65, 78–79
wells, 32, 44

wheat production, 83
windstorms, 33
women
    education and, 86
    modernization and, 16
    rights of, 55–56, 67, 101
    role of, 36
World War II, 71, 76

Yanbu, 73, 102
Yemen, 20, 26, 33
Yom Kippur War, 14

zinc, 82

About the Contributors

ROBERT A. HARPER is professor emeritus of geography, University of Maryland, College Park. He also taught at Southern Illinois University, Carbondale, and was a visiting professor at the University of Manchester, England; University of Sydney, Australia; University of Durban, South Africa; and Peking and Northwest Universities, China. He is past president of the National Council for Geographic Education and holds their George J. Miller Service Award and a Professional Achievement Award from his alma mater, the University of Chicago. He is the author, coauthor, or coeditor of geography texts that range from second grade to the university level. In retirement he has written *The University that Shouldn't Happen, BUT DID! Southern Illinois University during the Morris years 1948–1972*.

ASWIN SUBANTHORE is a geographer and teaching associate at Oklahoma State University. A native of Chennai, India, Subanthore's thematic research interest is cultural geography, with regional interests in South Asia, West Asia, and the Arab world. He is currently working on several scholarly works on the Middle East and South Asia.

CHARLES F. GRITZNER is distinguished professor of geography at South Dakota State University. He is now in his fifth decade of college teaching and research. Much of his career work has focused on geographic education. Gritzner has served as both president and executive director of the National Council for Geographic Education and has received the council's George J. Miller Award for Distinguished Service.